To: Thomas Hickey

Your work in the Lord's Kingdom through the years and your exemplary life is greatly appreciated and is (and has been) an encouragement to many.

Continue to be faithful in your life and in preaching the Word.

May God richly richly and keep and yours as long as you live.

Brotherly in Christ,
Carrol R. Sutton

MUST WE KEEP THE SABBATH TODAY?

What Do the *Scriptures* Teach?

Carrol Ray Sutton
1103 Edmondson Street
Albertville, Alabama 35950

ISBN: 0-9728625-0-1

Published
by

Tommy **Thrasher Publications**
1705 Sandra St. SW
Decatur, AL 35601

(256) 353-3085

Table of Contents

Table of Contents (Cont'd)

Foreword

God has revealed His marvelous truth in such a way that He intends for it to be studied and understood (2 Timothy 3:16-17; Ephesians 5:17). However, since the beginning of the church in the first century AD, issues have arisen that have divided those who claim to be the followers of Jesus Christ. Sincere seekers for truth have consistently confronted those questions by making their appeal to the Scriptures (Acts 17:11).

The proper role of the Sabbath day in worship and service to God has continued to be a major area of controversy among professed Christians. At least a dozen denominations, including Seventh-day Adventists, Seventh Day Baptists, the Church of God (Seventh Day), and the Worldwide Church of God, teach that the Sabbath day requirement of the Ten Commandments is still binding upon people in the New Testament age. Others contend that worship upon the first day of the week (Sunday) is the teaching of the New Testament. Regardless of the position taken, people recognize that this is an important issue. It can be properly settled only by what God has revealed.

Most of the material in this book originally appeared in *The Instructor*, a monthly periodical published by the East Albertville church of Christ, Albertville, Alabama. Carrol Sutton has served faithfully as editor since the first issue appeared in January 1964. To the best of my knowledge, *The Instructor* has been published for a longer period and has a greater circulation that any paper currently being published by a local church of Christ.

Brother Sutton has produced a complete answer to the arguments and positions of the Sabbatarians. As a faithful preacher of the gospel of Christ for more than fifty years, and a defender of the truth in numerous public de-

Foreword (Continued)

bates with proponents of error, brother Sutton has earned a reputation for clarity in presenting the teachings of the Book of God. His written articles are characterized by an easy-to-follow style that enables the reader to understand the points being made. More importantly, he does not neglect to give Bible proof for each argument.

In this book on the Sabbath, brother Sutton has clearly demonstrated the misapplications of Scripture, errors in argumentation, and failures of the Sabbatarians in setting forth proof for their theory. I commend this study to all who desire to learn the will of God on this question. May the Lord bless us in our search for His truth (John 8:32).

Thomas N. Thrasher
January 1, 2003

Preface

In His sermon on the mountain in Mt. 7:15-16 Jesus Christ warned his disciples to beware of false prophets. He said: **"Beware of false prophets, which come to you in sheep's clothing, but inwardly they are ravening wolves. Ye shall know them by their fruits..."** In Mt. 24:11 Jesus predicted that false prophets would come and deceive many when He said: **"And many false prophets shall rise, and shall deceive many."** Jesus warned His disciples to **"...Take heed that no man deceive you."** *We must take heed!*

We learn from Acts 13:6 that when Saul and Barnabas was on the isle of Cyprus and came to Paphos, **"they found a certain sorcerer, a false prophet, a Jew, whose name was Bar-jesus"**. Saul rebuked the false prophet and told him that the hand of the Lord was upon him and he would be blind for a season, and it happened. In 2 Cor. 11:13 –15 Paul referred to some as **"false apostles, deceitful workers."** Obviously they appeared as **"the ministers of righteousness"** but in reality *they were ministers of Satan. We must be vigilant!*

The apostle Peter warned of false teachers in 2 Peter 2:1-2 when he wrote: **"But there were false prophets also among the people, even as there shall be false teachers among you, who privily shall bring in damnable heresies, even denying the Lord that bought them, and bring upon themselves swift destruction. And many shall follow their pernicious ways; by reason of whom the way of truth shall be evil spoken of."** *We must be on guard!*

In view of the fact that in times past there *were* false prophets and today *there are false teachers,* it is obligatory that we heed the warnings of Jesus Christ, the apostle Paul and Peter as noted above and that we follow the admonition given by the apostle John. Listen to him: **"Beloved, believe not every spirit, but try the spirits whether they are of God: because many false prophets are gone out into the world."** (1 John 4:1). NOTE: John urges Christians to *"try"* that is, *test,*

7

Preface (Continued)

prove, examine. This must be done by using the Word of God as revealed in the Scriptures as our standard. Human traditions, doctrines and commandments of men, likes or dislikes, emotions do not qualify to serve as to our standard of authority. Jesus Christ has *all authority.*

The Holy Spirit revealed the Words of Christ to the apostles and they, in turn, preached it orally and wrote it down so others (and we) could have access to it in the Scriptures. (See Mt. 28:18; John 6:63; 14:26; 16:13-15; 1 Cor. 2:9-10; Eph. 3:2-6; 2 Tim. 3:16-17). Within the Scriptures we have God's truth and righteousness revealed.

The Hebrew writer exhorted Christians to **"Be not carried about with divers and strange doctrines."** (13:9). We find such expressions as *"the apostles' doctrine"*, *"the doctrine of the Lord'*, *"sound doctrine"*, *"good doctrine"*, *"the doctrine of God"*, *"the doctrine of Christ"*, and *"the doctrine which is according to godliness"* used in the New Testament to describe *the doctrine of Christ.* (See Acts 2:42; 13:12; Titus 2:1; 1 Tim. 4:6; Titus 2:10; 2 John 9; 1 Tim. 6:3). NOTE: Any doctrine that is contrary to **"the doctrine of Christ"** is a **"strange doctrine"**. *It is false!*

It is the belief of this writer that in the pages that follow it is clearly shown by the Scriptures that *the sabbath law* as contained in the covenant that God gave through Moses to Israel *is not binding on Christians in the Gospel Age.* Those who teach and promote "sabbath keeping" today are false teachers! I would like to urge every reader of this book to *receive the Word of God* with all readiness of mind, and **search the Scriptures daily to see if the things spoken within these pages are so**. (See Acts 17:11).

The Author
January 1, 2003

8

MUST WE KEEP THE SABBATH TODAY?

The sabbath is mentioned in the Scriptures more than 160 times. Although there is a lot of information given about the sabbath many people do not understand the truth regarding the sabbath.

There are a number of religious groups that teach that the sabbath should be kept or observed today as it was in Old Testament times. In view of this, a study of the question, "Must we keep the Sabbath today?" is justified and should prove helpful to many.

Our human traditions, preferences, likes or dislikes do not constitute the proper standard by which we can determine the truth about this subject. God's truth, as revealed in the Scriptures, is the standard by which we can determine God's will on this, as well as on all other religious subjects. Our appeal will be to the Scriptures.

I. WHAT DAY IS THE SABBATH? God has not left us to wonder or guess about what day is the sabbath. When God gave the ten commandments (not mere suggestions) He said: **"But the seventh day is the sabbath of the Lord thy God:..."** (Exo. 20:10 also see 31:15; Lev. 23:3; Dt. 5:14). NOTE: This settles it! *The seventh day, not the first, is the sabbath!*

II. WHO GAVE THE SABBATH LAW? It is obvious from a reading of the Scriptures that God gave the Sabbath law through Moses. In Exodus 20 and Deuteronomy 5 we have an account of the giving of the ten command-

9

ments which included the commandment to **"Remember the sabbath day, to keep it holy."** Deuteronomy 5:15 says: **"...therefore the Lord thy God commanded thee to keep the sabbath day."**

In their prayer to God (in Neh. 9:13-14) the Levites said: **"Thou camest down also upon mount Sinai, and spakest with them from heaven, and gavest them right judgments, and true laws, good statutes and commandments: And madest known unto them thy holy sabbath, and commandest them precepts, statutes, and laws, by the hand of Moses thy servant."**

We learn from John 1:17 that **"...the law was given by Moses, but grace and truth came by Jesus Christ."** Speaking to Jews, Jesus said: **"Did not Moses give you the law, and yet none of you keepeth the law? Why go ye about to kill me?"** (John 7:19). NOTE: The same law that said, **"Thou shalt not kill"** also said, **"Remember the sabbath day, to keep it holy."** Moses gave that law. We learn from Mt. 15:4 that **"God commanded, saying, Honour thy father and mother..."** and from Mark 7:10 that **"Moses said, Honour thy father and thy mother..."** NOTE: It is obvious from reading these two passages that Moses said what God commanded. *It necessarily follows that God gave the law (including the sabbath command) through Moses!*

III. TO WHOM WAS THE SABBATH LAW GIVEN? It was given to Israelites! Exodus 20:1-2 says: **"And God spake all these words, saying, I am the Lord thy God, which have brought thee out of the land of Egypt, out of the house of bondage."** Then the ten commandments were given (including the sabbath command). In Dt. 5:1-3 we read: **"And Moses called all Israel, and said unto them, Hear, O Israel, the statutes and judgments which I speak in your ears this day, that ye may learn them, and keep, and do**

10

them. The Lord our God made a covenant with us in Horeb. The Lord made not this covenant with our fathers, but with us, even us, who are all of us here alive this day." In verse 6 God said: "I am the Lord thy God, which brought thee out of the land of Egypt, from the house of bondage." In verse 12 He said: "Keep the sabbath day to sanctify it, as the Lord thy God hath commanded thee." In verse 15 God said: "And remember that thou was servant in the land of Egypt, and that the Lord thy God brought thee out thence through a mighty hand and by a stretched out arm: therefore the Lord thy God commanded thee to keep the sabbath day."

We learn from 1 Kings 8:9 that "There was nothing in the ark (of the covenant -ed.) save the two tables of stone, which Moses put there at Horeb, when the Lord made a covenant with the children of Israel, when they came out of the land of Egypt." The Lord told Moses to speak unto the children of Israel, saying: "Wherefore the children of Israel shall keep the sabbath, to observe the sabbath throughout their generations, for a perpetual covenant. It is a sign between me and the children of Israel for ever:..." (Exo. 31:16-17). NOTE: The evidence is clear! The proof is ample! The conclusion is irristible! *God through Moses gave the sabbath law to the children of Israel!*

IV. WHEN WAS THE SABBATH LAW GIVEN? The Israelites were first told to *"observe"* the sabbath just prior to the giving of the ten commandments at Sinai. (Cf. Exo. 16-20). The Levites (in their prayer to God) said: "Thou camest down also upon the mount Sinai, and spakest with them from heaven, and gavest them right judgments, and true laws, good statutes and commandments: And

11

madest known unto them thy holy sabbath, and commandest them precepts, statutes, and laws, by the hand of Moses thy servant." (Neh. 9:13-14). Also read and study Dt. 4:10-13. NOTE: The sabbath was *"enjoined"* on the Israelites at Sinai (Horeb)! *There is no Scriptural evidence that God ever commanded any one prior to this time to "Keep the sabbath"!*

V. WHY WAS THE SABBATH LAW GIVEN? Here are two basic reasons why the sabbath law was given.

1. *It was given because the Israelites were servants in Egypt and God brought them out!* In addressing Israel, Moses said: **"And remember that thou was a servant in the land of Egypt and that the Lord thy God brought thee out thence through a mighty hand and by a stretched out arm: therefore the Lord thy God commanded thee to keep the sabbath day."** (Dt. 5:15).

2. *It was given as a sign between God and the children of Israel!* Exodus 31:12-13 says: **"And the Lord spake unto Moses, saying, Speak thou also unto the children of Israel, saying, Verily my sabbaths ye shall keep: for it is a Sign between me and you throughout your generations; that ye may know that I am the Lord that doth sanctify you."** In verse 17 He said: **"It is a sign between me and the children of Israel for ever:..."** (Cf. Ezek. 20:12).

OBSERVATION: The sabbath law was *not* given universally to all peoples! It was limited in scope! To show proper respect for God and His Word we must limit the sabbath law to those to whom it was given! Yes, without question, the sabbath law was applicable to a certain group of people for a limited time!

VI. WHAT DID SABBATH KEEPING RE-QUIRE? Since God gave the command to the Israelites to

"**Remember the sabbath day, to keep it holy**" (Exodus 20:8), only God had the right to give the requirements of sabbath keeping. God gave some negative requirements and some positive ones. In fact God gave more negative than positive ones. Here are some things that He required of the Israelites.

1. *They were required to do no work on the sabbath!* He commanded them: "**Remember the sabbath day, to keep it holy. Six days, shalt thou labor and do all thy work: But the seventh day is the sabbath of the Lord thy God: in it thou shalt not do any work, thou, nor thy son, nor thy daughter, thy manservant, nor thy maidservant, nor thy cattle, nor thy stranger that is within thy gates: for in six days the Lord made heaven and earth, the sea, and all that in them is, and rested the seventh day: wherefore the Lord blessed the sabbath day, and hallowed it.**" (Exodus 20:8-10). In Exodus 31:15 the Lord spake through Moses, saying, "**Six days may work be done; but in the seventh is the sabbath of rest, holy to the Lord: whosoever doeth any work in the sabbath day, he shall surely be put to death.**" Again in Exodus: 35:2 we read: "**Six days shall work be done, but on the seventh day there shall be to you an holy day, a sabbath of rest to the Lord: whosoever doeth work therein shall be put to death.**"

In Numbers 15:32-36 we read: "**And while the children of Israel were in the wilderness, they found a man that gathered sticks upon the sabbath day. And they that found him gathering sticks brought him unto Moses and Aaron and unto all the congregation. And they put him in ward, because it was not declared what should be done to him. And the Lord said to Moses, The man shall be surely put to death: all the congregation shall stone him with stones without the camp. And all the congregation brought him without the camp, and stoned him with stones, and he died;**

13

as the Lord commanded Moses." The evidence is clear! The proof is ample! God required the Israelites to do no work on the sabbath! They were required to rest on the sabbath!

2. *They were required to do no baking or boiling on the sabbath!* When gathering the manna (bread) provided for them from heaven, they were to gather twice as much on the sixth day than on other days. The Lord through Moses said: **"Tomorrow is the rest of the holy sabbath unto the Lord: bake that which ye will bake to day, and seethe that ye will seethe; and that which remaineth over lay up for you to be kept until the morning."** (Exodus 16:23). It is obvious that Israelites were not to gather manna nor bake or boil any thing on the sabbath!

3. *They were required to kindle no fire on the sabbath!* The Israelites were clearly instructed, **"Ye shall kindle no fire throughout your habitations upon the sabbath day."** (Exodus 35:3). This instruction is plain and easily understood! Sabbath keeping required the kindling of no fires in their dwellings!

4. *They were required to bear no burden on the sabbath!* The Lord through Jeremiah commanded the Israelites, saying, **"Take heed to yourselves, and bear no burden on the sabbath day, nor bring it in by the gates of Jerusalem; neither carry forth a burden out of your houses on the sabbath day, neither do ye any work, but hallow ye the sabbath day, as I commanded your fathers."** (17:21-23). These instructions were given hundreds of years after the giving of the command to keep the sabbath day holy at Mount Sinai as recorded in Exodus 20. It is obvious that these same requirements had been given to their "fathers". Without question, the Israelites were required to bear no burden on the sabbath day!

14

5. *They were required to offer two lambs, etc. on the sabbath!* After discussing a number of other offerings we read in Numbers 28:9-10 that the Lord said, **"And on the sabbath day two lambs of the first year without spot, and two tenth deals of flour for a meat offering, mingled with oil, and the drink offering thereof: this is the burnt offering of every sabbath, beside the continual burnt offering, and his drink offering."** This offering (including two lambs) was required for sabbath keeping! *Yes, sabbath keeping required the offering of two lambs,* etc.

In view of the above requirements of the Israelites for sabbath keeping, if we examine the so-called "Christian" churches that claim to be keepers of the sabbath day we find their "sabbath keeping" lacking. They pick and choose what they want to practice for "sabbath keeping" without regard for the Scriptural requirements of the Israelites to whom the sabbath command was given! In other words, those who claim to be keeping the sabbath day holy do not observe the sabbath as the Israelites were told to observe it!

If we are to observe the sabbath day because it was one of the ten commandments given to Israel on Mount Sinai, it is imperative that we observe it by meeting the requirements of sabbath keeping as set forth in the above Scriptures!

VII. WHAT WAS THE PENALTY FOR VIOLATING THE SABBATH COMMAND TO DO NO WORK? The Lord told Moses to speak to the Israelites saying, **"Ye shall keep the sabbath therefore; for it is holy unto you: every one that defileth it shall surely be put to death: for whosoever doeth any work therein, that soul shall be cut off from among the people. Six days may work be done; but in**

15

the seventh is the sabbath of rest, holy to the Lord: whosoever doeth any work in the sabbath day, he shall surely be put to death." (Exodus 31:14-15). In Exodus 35:1-2 we read that "Moses gathered all the congregation of the children of Israel together, and said unto them, these are the words which the Lord hath commanded, that ye should do them. Six days shall work be done, but on the seventh day there shall be to you an holy day, a sabbath of rest to the Lord: whosoever doeth work therein shall be put to death." We learn from the above text that working on the sabbath defiled the sabbath and that the penalty was death. NOTE: For any person that worked on the sabbath the penalty was death. Rather severe, wasn't it?

In Numbers 15:32-36 we read that "...While the children of Israel were in the wilderness, they found a man that gathered sticks upon the sabbath day. And they that found him gathering sticks brought him unto Moses and Aaron, and unto all the congregation. And they put him in ward, because it was not declared what should be done to him. And the Lord said unto Moses, The man shall be surely put to death: all the congregation shall stone him with stones without the camp. And all the congregation brought him without the camp, and stoned him with stones, and he died; as the Lord commanded Moses." NOTE: Here is an example of a man being put to death because he had violated the sabbath law! What had he done? He gathered sticks upon the sabbath day.

If the sabbath law is binding on us today, it would necessarily follow that the penalty for violating it should be inflicted. If not, why not? Or could one violate the sabbath law and thus defile the sabbath with impunity? The first seven commandments (including the sabbath command) of the ten commandment law had death as the penalty for violating them. The last three could result in death or could lead to other violations and result in death. (Cf. Deut. 13:6-17;

16

Exodus 22:20; Lev. 24:10-16; Exodus 21:15; 21:12-14; Lev. 20:10; Exodus 22:1-14; 21:16; Deut. 19:16-21; Joshua 7; etc.) In fact the law (or covenant) that contained the ten commandments as given to the children of Israel was one of death! It also made provisions for death to be the penalty for a false prophet, witch, stubborn son, negligent owner of a goring ox, etc. (Cf. Deut. 13:5; Exodus 22:18; Deut. 21:18-21; Exodus 21:29; Numbers 1:51; etc.)

Not only did God give the children of Israel the covenant (or law) that contained certain commandments (and regulations) but He also gave them certain penalties that they were to administer for certain sins. If the covenant (or law) that contained the ten commandments that God gave to the Israelites is to be kept today, it would necessarily follow that the penalties for violating that law (or covenant) should be administered today. If not, why not? Do not allow those who refuse to exact the death penalty upon those who violate the sabbath law impose on you a partial keeping of that law. It is not wholly kept by them.

The law that God gave to the children of Israel not only contained the things mentioned above but it also required *circumcision* (Lev. 12:3; Joshua 5:2-9; John 7:22-23), *keeping the passover* (Lev. 9:1-5; Deut. 16:1-8), *the feast of tabernacles* (Lev. 23: 33-36), *the feast of weeks (or Pentecost)* (Deut. 16:9-11), etc.

The children of Israel were under the above requirements and regulations. These requirements and regulations were never intended to govern Christians. If Christians today are under one of the above requirements because they were given to the children of Israel, they are under all of them on the same basis! In Gal.3:10-12 Paul said, **"For as many as are of the works of the law are under**

17

the curse: for it is written, Cursed is every one that continueth not in all things which are written in the book of the law to do them. But that no man is justified by the law in the sight of God, it is evident: for, The just shall live by faith." In Gal. 5:2-3 Paul said, "Behold, I Paul say unto you, that if ye be circumcised, Christ shall profit you nothing. For I testify again to every man that is circumcised, that he is a debtor to do the whole law." NOTE: It is clear from these verses that we have no right to "pick and choose" as we please from the covenant (or law) that God gave through Moses to the children of Israel about 3500 years ago. If we take circumcision or the sabbath we are debtors to do the whole law! Paul also declared that **"Christ is become of no effect unto you, whosoever of you are justified by the law; ye are fallen from grace."** (Gal. 5:4). If a Christian tries to justify the practice of binding circumcision or sabbath keeping today by the law he has fallen from grace!

Do not allow those who are debtors to do the whole law to *deceive you* into thinking that we must keep the sabbath today!

THE SABBATH LAW IS NOT BINDING ON CHRISTIANS.

Several religious groups teach that the sabbath law is still binding and it is obligatory that Christians observe the sabbath. Others teach that it is not binding on Christians today. To answer the question our appeal must not be to traditions, emotions, preferences, likes or dislikes. Our appeal must be to the Scriptures in order to learn God's will in this as well as in other matters.

The sabbath law is no longer in force. It is not binding on Christians in the gospel age. Here are some passages that teach that the law (that contained the sabbath command) is no longer in force.

18

1. In Mt. 5:17-18 Jesus said: **"Think not that I am come to destroy the law, or the prophets: I am not come to destroy, but to fulfill. ...Till heaven and earth pass, one jot or one tittle shall in no wise pass from the law, till all be fulfilled ."** NOTE: Jesus did not come to destroy or to make the law void, but to *"fulfill"* it. Not one thing would pass from the law *"till"* (until) it accomplished what God intended it to accomplish! This implies that *"the law"* would pass when it was fulfilled! (Cf. Luke 24:44; Heb. 10:1-14).

2. In Col. 2:14-17 Paul said: **"Blotting out the handwriting of ordinances that was against us, which was contrary to us, and took it out of the way, nailing it to his cross; ...Let no man therefore judge you in meat, or in drink, or in respect of an holyday, or of the new moon, or of the sabbath days; Which are a shadow of things to come; but the body is of Christ."** NOTE: The ten commandment law was written **"with the finger of God."** As far as we know it is the only law that was written with the hand of God. (See Exo. 31:18; 24:12; 32:15-16). Jesus **"took it out of the way, nailing it to his cross!"**

3. In Eph. 2:14-16 Paul said: **"For he is our peace, who hath made both one, and hath broken down the middle wall of partition between us; Having abolished in his flesh the enmity, even the law of commandments contained in ordinances; for to make in himself of twain one new man, so making peace; And that he might reconcile both unto God in one body by the cross, having slain the enmity thereby."** NOTE: The **"law of commandments contained in ordinances"** was abolished when Jesus was nailed to the cross!

4. Rom.7: 4 says: **"Wherefore, my brethren, ye also are become dead to the law by the body of Christ; that ye should be married to another, even to him who is raised from**

19

the dead, that we should bring forth fruit unto God." NOTE: Paul said, "ye also are become dead to the law!" In verse 6 he also said: "But now we are delivered from the law..." To what law is Paul referring when he told the brethren that they were *"dead to the law"* and were *"delivered from the law?"* In verse 7 Paul clearly identifies that law as the ten commandment law when he said that he had not "known lust except the law had said, Thou shall not covet." This clearly identifies the law to which they were dead and from which they were delivered as the ten commandment law.

5. Hebrews 7:12 says: "For the priesthood being changed, there is made of necessity a change also of the law." NOTE: The people received the law under the Levitical priesthood. Jesus is now our high priest after the order of Melchisedec. He was not of the tribe of Levi and thus could not serve as priest under the law! Since the priesthood was changed there was made of necessity also a change of the law. We are not under the law given by Moses (which also contained the ten commandments), but we are under the law of Christ! The first covenant (which contained the ten commandments) is no longer in force. We are now subject to the new covenant of which Jesus Christ is the testator. It is a better testament (covenant) which was established upon better promises! (Cf. Heb. 7:11-22; 9:15-16; 8:7-13; 7:19). We are not under the Levitical priesthood and the law, but we are under the priesthood of Jesus Christ and *"grace and truth"*, the New Testament (covenant)!

6. In Gal. 3:24-25 we read: "Wherefore the law was our schoolmaster to bring us unto Christ, that we might be justified by faith. But after that faith is come, we are no longer under a schoolmaster." NOTE: The law was never intended to be permanent, but it was temporary and provi-

sional. It served to discipline, train and lead the Israelites unto Christ! It led them to the faith! After the faith was revealed the law was no longer needed for that purpose. The faith is the gospel of Christ! It is the power of God unto salvation to all true believers! (Cf. Rom. 1:16-18; Acts 6:7; Jude 3). We learn from verse 19 that the law was temporary. Paul stated that **"It was added because of transgressions till the seed should come..."**

When a person understands the nature and purpose of the law that God gave through Moses (including the ten commandments) to Israel, he will understand that it was provisional, and thus durational! It was intended primarily for the nation of Israel. It was never intended for Gentile nations!

Let us keep in mind the fact that the law was abrogated at the cross! (See Col. 2:14-17).

7. In 2 Cor. 3:6-16 we have a discussion of the New Testament and the Old Testament. The Old Testament is referred as *"the letter"* and the New Testament is referred to as *"the spirit"*. The Old Testament is spoken of as **"the ministration of death, written and engraven in stones"** and the New Testament is spoken of as **"the ministration of the spirit"**. The Old Testament is referred to as **"the ministration of condemnation"** and the New Testament as **"the ministration of righteousness"**.

Throughout the passage we see a contrast between the two testaments (covenants). Please consider the following facts.

1. Paul and others were made **"ministers of the new testament"**! They were not made ministers of **"the letter"**. They were made ministers of **"the spirit"**. The **"letter killeth, but the spirit giveth life."** (Verse 6).

21

2. The **"ministration of death"** was written and engraven in stones. (Verse 7). We read in Deut. 4:13 that Moses told Israel that the Lord declared unto them His covenant, which He commanded them to perform, **"...even ten commandments: and he wrote them upon two tables of stone."** Obviously this identifies that which was written and engraven in stones that was the **"ministration of death"** as God's covenant, the ten commandments. (Also cf. Exodus 32:15-16).

3. **"The ministration of death"** (the Old Covenant including the ten commandments) was **"glorious, so that the children of Israel could not stedfastly behold the face of Moses for the glory of his countenance; which glory was to be done away"** but **"the ministration of righteousness"** does **"exceed in glory"**. In fact, in comparison to the glory of the **"ministration of righteousness"** the Old Covenant (**"the ministration of condemnation "**) **"had no glory"**. The glory of the New Covenant far excels or surpasses the glory of the Old Covenant. (Verses 7-10; cf. Exodus 34:27-35).

4. In contrasting the Old and New Testaments, Paul said: **"For if that which is done away was glorious, much more that which remaineth is glorious."** (Verse 11). NOTE: Paul is teaching that the Old Covenant (spoken of as the **"ministration of condemnation"**, etc.) is **"done away"** and that the New Testament (spoken of as the **"ministration of righteousness"**, etc.) *remains!* This contrast is very clearly set forth here by the inspired apostle. Believe it!

5. That which **"was glorious"** which was **"done away"** was the **"ministration of death, written and engraven in stones"**. It was the Old Covenant (including the ten commandments) that God gave to Israel through Moses when

22

his face shone as recorded in Exodus 34:27-35. Paul referred to this in 2 Cor. 3.

6. The **"letter"**, (the **"ministration of death"**, the **"ministration of condemnation"**, **"that which was glorious"**, the **"old testament"**, **"Moses"**) was "done away" (i.e., **"abolished'**)! (Cf. 2 Cor.3: 6-17).

7. The **"spirit"**, (the **"ministration of the spirit"**, the **"ministration of righteousness"** (the **"new testament"**) **"remaineth "**!

It is clear from a study of 2 Cor. 3:6-18 that the Old Covenant (including the command to the Israelites to **"Remember the sabbath day, to keep it holy"** in Exodus 20:8) is not binding on Christians today! Accept it!

Now let us consider some syllogistic reasoning on the ten commandment law given by Moses to Israel and "sabbath keeping."

SYLLOGISMS

1. The ten commandments, written and engraven in stones, were glorious.   (For proof see Exodus 32:16; Deut. 4:13; 2 Cor. 3:7).

2. But that which was glorious was done away!   (See 2 Cor. 3:7, 11).

3. Therefore: *The ten commandments were done away*! (A logical conclusion.)

1.   The ten commandments were done away!
(Already proven)

2.   But the sabbath command is one of the ten commandments!   (See Exodus 20:8).

3. Therefore: *The sabbath command was done away*!   (A logical conclusion. It is inescapable!)

1.The covenant that God made with Israel when He brought them out of Egypt was (or included) the ten commandments!   (For proof see Deut. 4:13; 10:1-5; 1 Kings 8:9).

2. But God took away the covenant He made with Israel when He brought them out of Egypt.   (See Hebrews 8:6-13; 10:9).

3. Therefore: ***God took away the ten commandments* (one of which is the sabbath command)!** (A definite conclusion).

1. We are dead to the law that said, **"Thou shalt not covet"**.   (For proof see Romans 7:4-7).

2. But the ten commandment law said, **"Thou shalt not covet "**.   (See Exodus 20:17).

3. Therefore: ***We are dead to the ten commandment law***! (A sure conclusion).

1. We are dead to the ten commandment law!   (Proven above).

2. But the sabbath command is in the ten commandment law!   (See Exodus 20:8).

3. Therefore: ***We are dead to the sabbath command!***   (An inevitable conclusion).

SOME FACTS ABOUT THE TWO COVENANTS

Among the facts we can learn from a reading and study of Jeremiah 31:31-34 and Hebrews 8:6-13 are the following:

1. There are *two* covenants under consideration. They are the *first* covenant and the *second* covenant.

2. The *first* covenant is spoken of as being "*old*" and the *second* covenant is spoken of as being "*new*".

3. The *new* covenant is *not* according to the *first* or *old* covenant!

4. The *first* covenant was not faultless! Heb. 8:7 says: **"For if that first covenant had been faultless, then should no place have been sought for the second."** NOTE: The fact that the Israelites broke that covenant does not prove that the first covenant was not faulty!

5. The fact that God said **"a new covenant"** indicates that **"He has made the first old** (*obsolete* - NKJV)." (See Heb. 8:13).

6. Jesus Christ is the mediator of the *second* (or *new*) covenant!

7. The *new* (or *second*) is **"a better covenant, which was established upon better promises"**!

8. In making a *new* covenant the Lord made the *first* covenant *old* and it would vanish away.

Many people fail to properly divide the Word of God because they fail to recognize the *distinctions* between the *two covenants*.

ADDITIONAL FACTS ABOUT THE TWO COVENANTS

Let us now consider some additional facts about the *two covenants*.

9. The first covenant referred to as **"the law"** in a number of passages **"was given by Moses"** but the *second covenant* (included in the expression, **"truth and grace"** in John 1:17) **"came by Jesus Christ"**! (Cf. Gal. 6:2). (Of course, God gave *"the law"* to Israel through Moses).

10. The *first covenant* was given at Mt. Sinai, but the *second covenant* went forth from Jerusalem! (Cf. Neh. 9:13-14; Exodus 19 & 20; Isaiah 2:2-4; Luke 24:47; Acts 1:8).

11. The *first covenant* was given to the Israelites, but the *second* (also referred to as the *gospel*) was given to all, to Gentiles as well as to Israelites. (Cf. Deut. 5:1-3; Mark 16:15-16; Mt. 28:18-20; Eph. 2:11-16).

12. The *first covenant* contained the **ten commandments** (Exo. 34:28), **sacrifices** (cf. Deut. 12:6-11), **burnt offerings** (cf. Exo. 29:16-18), **incense** (cf. Exo. 30:1, 7-8; Luke 1:8-9), etc. In the *second* (or *new*) *covenant* we learn of **Christ's sacrificial death on the cross to atone for the sins of the world, His burial and resurrection** (cf. I Cor. 15:1-4), **the church that He built** (cf. Mt. 16:18; Col. 1:18; Eph. 5:23-25), **how to be saved from past sins** (cf. Luke 24:47; Rom. 10:9-10; Mark 16:15-16; Eph. 2:8-9), **how to worship** and **serve God** (cf. John 4:24; Heb. 12:28), **how to live** (cf. Titus 2:11-12), etc.

13. The *first covenant* was dedicated (or inaugurated) with **animal blood** (cf. Exo. 24:3-8), but the *second covenant* required the *blood of Christ* before it could be put into force (cf. Heb. 9:11-26; Mt. 26:28). For a testament to be in effect there must first be the death of the testator (cf. Heb. 9:15-16).

14. Under the *first covenant* there was a yearly remembrance of sins (cf. Heb. 10:3), but under the *second covenant* the Lord said, **"And their sins and iniquities will I remember no more"** (Heb. 10:16-17).

15. The *first covenant* was *faulty* (cf. Heb. 8:7), but the *second covenant* is *perfect* (cf. Heb. 7:19; James 1:25).

16. The *first covenant* (referred to as "the law") was to be in force *until* **"the seed"** (Christ) came (cf. Gal. 3:19-29), but the *second covenant* (the words of Christ as contained in the gospel) was to last till the end of the world (cf. Mt. 28:18-20; Mt. 24:35; John 12:48).

17. The *first covenant* was taken away that the *second* might be established! The Hebrew writer declared that **"He taketh away the first, that he may establish the second"** (10:9-10; cf. 9:16-17). NOTE: Obviously, both covenants could not be in force simultaneously. One would be in force at a time. The first was taken away that the second could be established. Since the second has been established it is obvious that the first has been taken away. Simple! Will you accept this truth?

18. A change of the priesthood necessitated a change also of the law. The Hebrew writer declared: **"For the priesthood being changed, there is made of necessity a change also of the law."** (7:12). Under the *first covenant* only those who were descendants of Levi could serve as priests. In fact, reference is made in Heb. 7:11 to the **"Levitical"** priesthood. It was under that priesthood that the people received the law (the *first covenant*). However, Jesus was not of the tribe of Levi, but of the tribe of Judah. Jesus could not have become priest under the Levitical priesthood, but He did become priest! He became priest after the order of Melchisedec. Under the *first covenant* He could not have become a priest! This change of priesthood necessitated also a change of the law! Jesus still serves as our Priest. He not only serves as our Priest, but He serves as our High Priest! There is no doubt about it. *We are not under the first* (i.e., *old*) *covenant, but we are under the second (i.e., new) covenant!* (Cf. Heb. 7:11-28).

27

19. The Israelites are dead to the *first covenant* (the law that said **"thou shalt not covet"**) that they might be married to Christ under the *second* (new) *covenant*! In Romans 7:4 Paul said: **"Wherefore, my brethren, ye also are become dead to the law by the body of Christ; that ye should be married to another, even to him who is raised from the dead, that we should bring forth fruit unto God."** NOTE: If we are not dead to that law then we could not be and thus we are not married to Christ. We learn from verse 6 that Paul said, **"But now we are delivered from the law, that being dead wherein we were held; that we should serve in newness of spirit, and not in the oldness of the letter."** NOTE: The law to which we are dead is the same law from which we have been delivered. Plain, isn't it?

20. Under the *first covenant* the Gentiles were dead in sins without God and Christ. (Cf. Eph. 2:1-12). Under the *second covenant* the Gentiles can be quickened and made alive. They can have both God and Christ. (Cf. Eph. 2:1-12; 2 John 9). Under the *first covenant* the Gentiles were afar off, aliens, strangers and foreigners and without hope. However, under the *second covenant* the Gentiles could be made nigh, fellow citizens with the saints and have hope (Cf. Eph. 2:12-19; Romans 15:13).

21. We cannot be justified by the works of the law (*first* covenant), but we can be justified by **"the faith of Jesus Christ"** (the *second* or *new* covenant)! (Cf. Gal 2:16).

22. We fall from grace if we try to be justified by the law (*first* covenant). We are justified by **"the faith"** (*second* covenant). We are **"under law to Christ"** (Cf. Gal. 5:4; Gal. 3:23-27; 1 Cor. 9:21). We must obey the teachings of Jesus Christ. (Cf. 2 John 9-11).

ARGUMENTS FOR SABBATH KEEPING EXAMINED

Some who teach that Christians should keep the sabbath holy as taught in the Old Testament Scriptures will make the following arguments in an effort to prove that Christians today should keep the sabbath holy as required of the Israelites under the Old Testament Scriptures. We are going to list the arguments that we've heard Sabbatarians make and then give a reply for your consideration.

1. "GOD RESTED ON THE SEVENTH DAY AND BLESSED AND SANCTIFIED IT."
   REPLY:
   (1) According to Gen. 2:2-3 God did rest on the seventh day and "blessed" and "sanctified" it. However, there is no *Scriptural proof* that God commanded or authorized anyone to keep the sabbath day holy until after the Israelites were delivered from the bondage of Egypt. The "sabbath" day is first mentioned in Exodus 16:23. A short time later God gave the ten commandments at Mt. Sinai (or Mt. Horeb). (Cf. Exodus 20:1-23; Deuteronomy 5:1-22).

   (2) The fact that God blessed the seventh day does not prove that Christians should keep the sabbath today! God blessed Adam and Eve (cf. Gen. 1:28; 5:1-2) and Potiphar's house (cf. Gen. 39:5) but that doesn't prove anything necessarily about what Christians are to do.

   (3) The fact that God sanctified the seventh day is no proof that Christians should keep the sabbath! God sanctified (hallowed) *the tabernacle* and *all things therein* (cf. Exodus 29:44; Lev. 8:10), *the firstborn of children of Israel, both man and beast,* (cf. Numbers 8:17), *a fast* (cf. Joel 1:14), and *Solomon's temple* (cf. 2 Chron. 7:16).

29

(4) We do not learn from Gen. 2:2-3 when God blessed and sanctified the seventh day! Moses (probably writing 2500 years after the creation) simply states the fact that God blessed and sanctified the seventh day without telling us *when* He did so!

(5) Gen. 2:2-3 says: **"And on the seventh day God ended his work which he had made; and he rested on the seventh day from all his work which he had made. And God blessed the seventh day and sanctified it; because in it he had rested from all his work which God created and made."** NOTE: The text tells us that God blessed and sanctified (past tense) the seventh day and it tells us *why* he did, but it does not tell us *when* He did so! Sabbatarians assume and assert without proof that Christians should keep the sabbath today!

2. "THE SABBATH WAS OBSERVED BY ADAM."
REPLY:
(1) An assumption pure and simple! No proof!
(2) Even if it could be proven that Adam observed the sabbath, that would not prove that Christians today should observe it! Adam was commanded to dress and keep the garden of Eden (cf. Gen. 2:15), but this does not prove that we must do so!
(3) We are not under law to Adam, but we are under the law to Christ! (Cf. 1 Cor. 9:21).

3. "ABRAHAM OBSERVED THE SABBATH BECAUSE GEN. 26:5 SAYS: 'BECAUSE THAT ABRAHAM OBEYED MY VOICE, AND KEPT MY CHARGE, MY COMMANDMENTS, MY STATUTES, AND MY LAWS.' "
REPLY:

(1) The text says absolutely nothing about the sabbath or the ten commandments!

(2) God has given different commandments to different people at different times for different reasons. For example, God commanded Adam, saying, **"...Thou shalt not eat of it..."** (Gen. 2:17). In Gen. 6:14 Noah was commanded to **"Make thee an ark of gopher wood..."** (along with other commands). Gen. 6:22 says: **"And thus did Noah; according to all that God commanded him, so did he."**
NOTE: These commandments that Noah kept had absolutely nothing to do with the ten commandments.

(3) Here are some of the things that God commanded Abraham to do.

A. Leave his country and kinsman and go into a land that God would show him. (Cf. Gen. 12:1-5).

B. Walk through the land of Canaan and observe it. (Cf. Gen. 13:12-17).

C. Keep the covenant of circumcision. (Cf. Gen. 17:9-14).
D. Hearken unto Sarah and cast out the bondwoman (Hagar) and her son. (Gen. 21:9-12).

E. Offer Isaac for a burnt offering. (Cf. Gen.22:1-2). NOTE: Abraham was obeying God's voice and keeping God's commandments when he did what God told him to do. It was not necessary for him to keep the sabbath to be obeying the commandments of God since there is no proof that God ever commanded him to keep it!

4. "THE SABBATH IS SPOKEN OF AS THE

31

HOLY SABBATH."

REPLY:

(1) Yes, Nehemiah 9:13-14 and Exo. 16:23 mentions **"holy sabbath"**. However, this does not prove that Christians should keep the sabbath today.

(2) We learn from Exo. 28:2 that Moses was to **"...make holy garments for Aaron..."**

(3) The Israelites were to have **"an holy anointing oil"** and a perfume that was **"pure and holy"**. (Cf. Exo. 30:25, 34-37).

(4) The tabernacle and the vessels therein were **"holy"**. (Cf. Exo. 40:9; 1 Kings 8:4). QUESTION: Must Christians have holy garments, anointing oil, perfume, a tabernacle and the vessels as the Israelites were required to do? Surely not.

(5) The firstling of a cow, a sheep or a goat could not be redeemed because it was **holy** according to Numbers 18:17.

In view of the above information we must conclude that the fact that the sabbath was spoken of as holy does *not* prove that Christians should keep it holy!

5."THE SABBATH IS A UNIVERSAL DAY OF WORSHIP FOR ALL MANKIND."

REPLY:

(1) A pure assumption! An assumption in not proof. Where is the Scriptural proof?

(2) As pointed out in previous studies, the command to keep the sabbath day holy was given to the Israelites for specific reasons and was never give to govern all mankind for all ages!

(3) Please note that Moses was speaking to "**all Israel**" (not to all mankind) when he gave the sabbath command according to Deut. 5:1-22. That settles it!

(4) There is absolutely no Scriptural proof that God ever intended that the sabbath law be universal in application.

We have examined five arguments that are sometimes made in an effort to prove that the sabbath is binding on Christians today. Before continuing, here is one additional thought about the argument that "*The sabbath was observed by Adam.*" If he kept the sabbath it was not because it was one of the ten commandments. He did not keep the ten commandments! Adam could not have kept all ten commandments because he had no father and mother to honor as required by the fifth commandment. We must conclude that the ten commandments were not given to Adam! Let us now continue our study.

6. "GOD BLESSED THE SABBATH DAY."
REPLY:

(1) Yes, God blessed the sabbath according to Gen. 2:3 and Exo. 20:11. However, this does not prove that Christians should keep the sabbath day holy as God required the Israelites to do. We should not assume and assert that it does!

(2) Referring to Potiphar Gen. 39:5 says; "**...The Lord blessed the Egyptian's house for Joseph's sake; and the blessing of the Lord was upon all that he had in the house and in the field.**" However, this does not prove that Potiphar will be saved eternally. Neither does it prove that God has blessed your house. Do we need to be in Potiphar's house in order to be blessed today? Of course not!

33

7. "GOD HALLOWED OR SANCTIFIED THE SAB-BATH DAY."
REPLY

(1) There are a number of things that are spoken of as ***being hallowed or sanctified***. Here are some of them: *the tabernacle and vessels* (Exo. 40:9; Lev. 8:10), *the firstborn* (Numbers 3:13; 8:17), *the temple* (1 Kings 9:3), *censers* (Numbers 16:37), *the fiftieth year* (Lev. 25:10), and *Aaron and his garments* (Exo. 29:21). NOTE: The fact that these things were hallowed or sanctified does not prove that we as Christians should provide, build and use them as they were used under the law. Is there any Sabbatarian who believes we should?

(2) Yes, God hallowed or sanctified the sabbath according to Exo. 20:11 and Gen. 2:3. However, this does not prove that Christians should keep the sabbath holy anymore than the fact that God hallowed or sanctified those other things mentioned above proves that we must provide, build and use those things in worship to God today under the New Covenant that God provided through Jesus Christ!

8. "GOD REFERRED TO THE SABBATH AS 'MY HOLY DAY' ".
REPLY:

(1) The fact that God referred to the sabbath as "**my holy day**" (in Isaiah 58:13) under the Old Covenant for the Israelites ***does not prove*** that the sabbath is God's holy day under the New Covenant for Christians.

(2) It is also a fact that under the Old Covenant that God referred to "**...my holy things, in the most holy place...**" (Ezekiel 44:13). However, this does not prove that those

34

things that were God's holy things under the First Covenant are God's holy things under the New Covenant and that Christians ought to recognize them as being God's holy things now and use them as such!

(3) Things that were considered **"holy"** and things that were considered **"most holy"** under the Old Covenant should not be *so* recognized and used today unless Christ authorized such in the New Testament! We should **"speak"** and **"do"** as they that **"shall be judged by the law of liberty!"** (James 2:12).

9. "THE SABBATH WAS TO BE OBSERVED 'THROUGHOUT THEIR GENERATIONS'"

REPLY:

(1) Yes, the sabbath was to be observed **"throughout their generations"** according to such passages as Exodus 31:13-16. Please note that the antecedent of **"their"** is "the children of Israel" (See verse 16). In view of this fact we can clearly see that the children of Israel were to observe the sabbath throughout their generations!

(2) Aaron was to make an atonement with animal blood for a sin offering once a year throughout their generations! (Cf. Exodus 30:10). NOTE: Does this fact prove that Christians today should be making an atonement with animal blood for a sin offering once a year? Of course not!

(3) Incense was to be burned before the Lord throughout their generations! (Cf. Exodus 30:7-8).

QUESTION: Does this prove that Christians should be burning incense before the Lord continually as the Israelites did? Of course not! If the sabbath is binding on us because of the expression, then why not burning incense?

35

(4) The children of Israel were told to make **"fringes on the borders of their garments throughout their generations"**. (Cf. Numbers 15:38). QUESTION: Does this prove that Christians should make fringes on the borders of their garments today? Of course not!

(5) Every honest person should easily see the fact that the Israelites were to keep the sabbath holy "throughout their generations" does not prove that the sabbath law is binding on Christians! NOTE: The expression **"throughout their generations"** as used there does not include *the Gospel Age*!

10. "THE SABBATH LAW WAS A PERPETUAL COVENANT".
    REPLY:

(1) Yes, according to Exodus 31:16 the children of Israel were **"to observe the sabbath throughout their generations for a perpetual covenant."** However, this does not prove that the sabbath is to be observed by Christians for a perpetual covenant!

(2) The priests' office would be Aaron's and his sons **"for a perpetual statute"** according to Exodus 29:9, but this was not intended to show that Aaron and his sons would be holding the office of priest in the gospel age!

(3) In Ezekiel 46:14 we read of **"a meat offering continually by a perpetual ordinance unto the Lord"**. However, this is no evidence or proof that Christians should be offering a meat offering continually today.

(4) The fact that the Levites were to be told that **"the field of the suburbs of their cities may not be sold; for it is their perpetual possession"** (Lev. 25:34) has absolutely

36

nothing to do with whether or not Christians have a right to sell their possessions? We can see that clearly, can't we?

11. "THE SABBATH WAS TO BE A SIGN FOR-EVER."
REPLY:

Yes, according to Exo. 31:17 it is so stated. However, that passage says a sign between the children of Israel and God! Not a sign between Christians and God. The word *forever* as used here means **"age lasting."** Also consider Exodus 31:16.

12. "THE ISRAELITES WERE KEEPING THE SABBATH IN EGYPT BECAUSE EXODUS 5:5 SAYS (Pharaoh speaking) **"...ye make them rest from their burdens."**
REPLY:

(1) The word from which rest comes simply means "to cause to cease, to hinder, to forbid" according to the *"Hebrew And English Lexicon"* by Gesenius. It does not mean that they were observing the sabbath! They had simply quit their work or ceased from their burdens. The context clearly indicates this. Read it carefully. We should never assume that every time the word *rest* is used it means the sabbath.

(2) A close reading of Ezekiel 20:10-12 will show that God did not give the Israelites His sabbaths until after they were brought out of Egypt.

(3) A study of Neh. 9:13-14 and Exodus 16 through 20 is further proof that they were not keeping the sabbath in Egypt!

(4) Even if the Israelites did keep the sabbath in Egypt this would not prove that the sabbath law is binding

on Christians!

13. "GOD'S PEOPLE OF ALL NATIONALITIES, WHETHER JEW OR GENTILE WERE DUTY BOUND TO OBSERVE THE SABBATH BECAUSE ISAIAH 56:6 SAYS: '**ALSO THE SONS OF THE STRANGER** (Gentile-CRS) **THAT JOIN THEMSELVES TO THE LORD....THAT KEEPETH THE SABBATH...' "**
REPLY:

(1) Of course the Gentiles who "**joined themselves to the Lord**" (accepted "the Jews' religion") kept the sabbath, but this fact does not prove that the sabbath is binding on "Christians"!

(2) We learn from Exo. 12:48 that the "stranger that would sojourn with the Israelites and "keep the passover of the Lord" was told to "**...let all his males be circumcised...for no uncircumcised person shall eat thereof."** (Also read and consider Exo. 20:10 & Ezekiel 44:9.) NOTE: It is obvious that when Gentiles "**joined themselves to the Lord**" they ceased being Gentiles and became proselytes to the Jewish religion. They then would keep the sabbath, but not then as Gentiles, but as Jews (or as Jewish proselytes). "**The stranger within thy gates**", not those "*without thy gates*" were the ones who were required to keep the sabbath, etc. FURTHER NOTE: The fact that God required the stranger who would sojourn with the Israelites to be circumcised does not prove that circumcision is binding on Christians.

(3) I know of no passage that required the Gentiles, as Gentiles, to keep the sabbath day holy. Even if we could find such a passage that would not prove that the sabbath is binding on Christians. Today, we live under the New Covenant of Jesus Christ!

38

14. "IN MARK. 2:27-28 JESUS SAID: **'THE SAB-BATH WAS MADE FOR MAN, AND NOT MAN FOR THE SABBATH: THEREFORE THE SON OF MAN IS LORD ALSO OF THE SABBATH.'"**
REPLY:

(1) Yes, Jesus said that but **He did not say** *"Therefore the sabbath law will be binding on Christians."* That is what "Sabbatarians" claim after reading the passage.

(2) Of course, the sabbath was made for man. In fact we learn as we study the Scriptures what man it was made for - the Israelite! It was made known to the Israelite after he came out of Egypt! (Cf. Ezekiel 20:10-12; Neh. 9:13-14 & Exodus 16 & 20).

(3) Contextually, Jesus was showing that their criticism of His disciples because they plucked ears of corn (and ate - Mt. 12:1) on the sabbath was improper because man was not made for the sabbath and that He (Jesus) was LORD even of the sabbath!

(4) Keep in mind that Jesus was living under the *Old Covenant* dispensation at the time He made the statement. There is nothing in His statement that proves that the sabbath would be binding on Christians under the *New Testament* dispensation!

15."THE TEN COMMANDMENTS HAVE AL-WAYS BEEN THE STANDARD OF RIGHT AND WRONG."
REPLY:

(1) An assertion based on assumption! No reliable evidence is given to prove this assertion! Truth seeking people demand evidence to prove such.

(2) There is no Scriptural proof that the ten commandments as such were given prior to the exodus of the children of Israel from Egypt. We know they were *not given* to Adam and Eve. One of the ten commandments says **"Honour thy father and thy mother..."** (Exo. 20:12), but Adam and Eve had no "father and mother" they could honour.

(3) Some of the sons of Kohath were told to not **"touch any holy thing, lest they die."** (Num. 4:15). If a person touched any holy thing he could be put to death. (Cf. Lev. 4:15). None of these things were a part of the ten commandments. However, they were a part of God's standard of right and wrong!

(4) The ten commandments were a part of (but not the whole of) God's standard of right and wrong! Now we are **"under the law to Christ"**! (Cf. 1 Corinthians 9:21).

16. "JESUS KEPT THE SABBATH."
REPLY:

(1) We learn from Luke 4:16-21 **"...And as his custom was, he** (Jesus-ed.) **went into the synagogue on the sabbath day, and stood up for to read..."** NOTE: The fact that Jesus may have or did keep the sabbath does not mean that the sabbath law is binding on Christians!

(2) We learn from Luke 2:21 that Jesus was circumcised the eighth day as required under the law, but that does not mean that circumcision is binding on Christians!

(3) We learn from Luke 22:1-20 that Jesus observed the Passover with His disciples, but this does not prove that the Passover is binding on Christians today.

40

(4) To understand why that Jesus kept the sabbath, was circumcised and observed the Passover we must consider the fact that He was **"made under the law."** (Cf. Gal. 4:4). Jesus lived under the law that required circumcision, the Passover and sabbath keeping, but Christians are not under that law!

17. "JESUS SAID 'NOT ONE JOT OR TITTLE WILL PASS FROM THE LAW TILL HEAVEN AND EARTH PASS AWAY.'"
REPLY:

(1) Jesus did not say what is stated in the above argument! Jesus did say: **"Think not that I am come to destroy the law, or the prophets: I am not come to destroy, but to fulfill...Till heaven and earth pass, one jot or one tittle shall in no wise pass from the law, till all be fulfilled."** (Mt. 5:17-18) NOTE: Jesus did not say that no part of the law would pass as long as heaven and earth remain, but he declared that as long as heaven and earth remain no part of the law would pass **"till all be fulfilled!"** A big difference!

(2) Compare the statement in Mt. 1:24-25 that **"...Joseph...took unto him his wife: And knew her not till she had brought forth her firstborn son: and he called his name Jesus."** NOTE: It is necessarily implied that Joseph *did know her* after Jesus was born. Likewise, no part of the law passed **"till all was fulfilled!"** However, when all was fulfilled the law passed away! Christ fulfilled the law! FURTHER NOTE: Since no part of the law (including animal sacrifices) would pass **"till all be fulfilled"**, we must conclude that no part of the law (including animal sacrifices) has passed away or that all the law (including the ten commandments) has passed away! If the law has

41

been fulfilled (and it has), then all the law (including the ten commandments) passed away! (Cf. John 19:30; Luke 24:44-48; Col. 2:14-17; Rom. 10:4; 7:4-7).

18. "IN MT. 24:20 JESUS TOLD THE DISCIPLES TO PRAY THAT THEIR FLIGHT BE NOT ON THE SABBATH DAY. THE EVENT THAT CAUSED THEM TO FLEE OCCURRED IN ABOUT AD 70, WHICH WAS ABOUT FORTY YEARS AFTER THE CRUCIFIXION. THIS PROVES THAT CHRISTIANS WOULD BE KEEPING THE SABBATH AT THAT TIME."
REPLY:

(1) Yes, Jesus told His disciples to **"pray ye that your flight be not in the winter, neither on the sabbath day"** in Mt. 24:20. However, this does not prove that the sabbath day is holy nor that Christians should observe the sabbath! NOTE: If this passage proves that the sabbath day is holy and that Christians should observe the sabbath in some special way, it would also prove that winter is a holy season and that Christians should observe winter in some special way! If not, why not?

(2) Jesus did not instruct his disciples to pray that their flight be not in the winter, neither on the sabbath day *because* they would be keeping the sabbath. That is wishful thinking on the part of Sabbatarians! They have good imaginations when it comes to sabbath keeping. In the very next verse Jesus told the disciples why they should pray that their flight not be in the winter nor on the sabbath day. He said: **"For then shall be great tribulation, such as was not since the beginning of the world to this time, no, nor ever shall be."**
It would be more difficult to flee on the sabbath since the gates of Jerusalem would be shut on the sabbath day! (See Nehemiah 13:19). NOTE: Obviously, Jesus had the safe-

ty of the disciples in mind and not the sacredness of the sabbath day when he made the above statement.

The statement of Jesus in Mt. 24:20 does not prove at all that Christians would or should keep the sabbath day!

19. "PAUL OBSERVED THE SABBATH DAY. HE PREACHED ON AT LEAST 76 SABBATH DAYS."
REPLY:

(1) It is an assumption and an assertion that Paul observed the sabbath day after his conversion! Evidence that proves this *is lacking*!

(2) There is no Scriptural proof that the apostle Paul (as a Christian) ever kept the sabbath day holy. It is certainly true that Paul often went into the synagogues on the sabbath day and preached. Immediately after his conversion, Paul **"preached Christ in the synagogues, that he is the Son of God"**. (Acts 9:20). In fact, he **"confounded the Jews which dwelt at Damascus, proving that this is very Christ"** according to Acts 9:22. In Thessalonica, where there was a synagogue of the Jews, **"Paul, as his manner was, went in unto them, and three sabbath days reasoned with them out of the scriptures..."** (Acts 17:2). In Berea Paul likewise went into the synagogue of the Jews and preached the Word of God. (See Acts 17:10-13). In Corinth Paul **"reasoned in the synagogue every sabbath, and persuaded the Jews and the Greeks."** (Acts 18:4). However, the fact that Paul went into the Jewish synagogues and preached God's Word does not prove that Paul kept the sabbath day holy.

(3) The fact I go into a Jewish synagogue on the sabbath and preach the Word of God is certainly no evidence that I am keeping the sabbath day holy as it was ob-

served by the children of Israel! NOTE: If a Sabbatarian goes into a pagan city and preaches, does that prove that he is observing pagan rituals? Of course not! See the point?

20. "THERE WERE TWO DISTINCT LAWS GIVEN TO THE ISRAELITES. ONE WAS 'THE TEN COMMANDMENTS' CALLED THE 'LAW OF GOD" AND THE OTHER WAS THE OLD LAW OF PARDON WHICH WAS THE 'LAW OF MOSES'. THE 'LAW OF MOSES' (OLD LAW OF PARDON WITH ITS SACRIFICES, ETC.) WAS NAILED TO THE CROSS, BUT 'THE LAW OF GOD' (THE TEN COMMANDMENTS) WAS NOT NAILED TO THE CROSS."

REPLY:

(1) The above argument is assumed and asserted, but the Scriptures do not prove it. Proof that two distinct laws were given at Sinai to the Israelites *must be proven* for the argument to be valid. We can read **"For if that first covenant had been faultless, then should no place have been sought for the second."** (Heb. 8:7). In Heb. 9:15-16 we can read about **"the new testament"** and **"the first testament"** (or covenant) and in Heb. 8:8-13 we read about a **"new covenant"** and an **"old."** Obviously, the first covenant and the old were one and the same. The **"new testament"** and **"the second"** are one and the same.

(2) There were two distinct testaments (covenants) given, but for two distinct dispensations. Nearly two thousand years ago the Hebrew writer (speaking of the first covenant) said: **"Now that which decayeth and waxeth old Is ready to vanish away."** (8:13). Contextually, reference is made to the covenant that the Lord made with the Israelites when he took them by the

44

hand to lead them out of the land of Egypt. The **"new testament (covenant)"** is the **"second"**. It is in contrast to **"the first"** which is **"old"**. It is not the *"third"*. It is **"the second"**! NOTE: If there were "two distinct laws" (or testaments) given at Sinai to the Israelites, then the New Testament of Jesus Christ would not be **"the second"** but it would be *"the third"*!

(3) The idea that **"the ten commandments"** were called **"the law of God"** (the Lord) *in contrast* with the old law of pardon with its sacrifices, etc. being called **"the law of Moses"** is merely an assumption and assertion without Scriptural proof.

(4) The fact that sometimes **"the ten commandments"** were called the law of God (or the Lord) does not mean that the other commandments and provisions given by the Lord are not a part of **"the law of the Lord."**

(5) The fact that sometimes **"the ten commandments"** may be called the law of Moses does not mean that the other commandments and provisions given by Moses are not a part of **"the law of Moses."**

(6) God gave the law of Moses! Ezra **"was a ready scribe in the law of Moses, which the Lord God of Israel had given..."** (Ezra 7:6; Cf. Neh. 8:1). NOTE: The law was called the law of Moses because God gave it through Moses!

(7) Without question, the law that Moses gave was God's law! Nehemiah 10:29 mentions **"...God's law, which was given by Moses the servant of God..."** We also read in 2 Chron. 34:14 that **"...Hilkiah the priest found a book of the law of the Lord given by Moses."** NOTE: God's law that Moses gave did not originate with Moses. It originated with God.

45

(8) Without question, Moses gave the ten commandments. In Mark 7:10 Jesus said: **"For Moses said, Honour thy father and thy mother..."** Observe the fact that Jesus did not say, *"For **God** said. Honour thy father and thy mother"* but He said: **"For *Moses* said, Honour..."** NOTE: This was one of the ten commandments that Moses gave!

In John 7:19 Jesus said: **"Did not Moses give you the law, and yet none of you keepeth the law? Why go ye about to kill me?"** NOTE: In going about to kill Jesus they were going about to violate the law that said: **"Thou shalt not kill."** That was one of the ten commandments and Moses gave the law that said that! Jesus said so!

(9) A careful reading of Nehemiah 8 will indicate that the expressions **"the book of the law of Moses"**, (v. 1), **"the law"** (v. 2, 7, 9, 13), **"the book of the law"** (v. 3), **"the book"** (v. 5), **"the book in the law of God"** (v.8), **"the law which the Lord had commanded by Moses"** (v. 14), and **"the book of the law of God"** (v. 18) are used interchangeably; therefore, referring to the same law!

(10) The "law of the Lord" contained information about **"burnt offerings for the sabbaths, and for the new moons, and for the set feasts..."**, *sacrifices,* etc. and *acts of Josiah* and *his goodness* (Cf. 2 Chron. 31:3; 35:26 & Lk. 2:23-24).

No, God did not give two distinct laws to Israel at Sinai! The idea that He did is born of human desire. God's will is expressed in His Word!

21. "HEBREW'S 4:9 TEACHES THAT CHRIST-IANS SHOULD KEEP THE SEVENTH DAY SABBATH HOLY BECAUSE IT SAYS: **'There remaineth therefore a rest to the people of God.'"**

REPLY:

(1) Sabbatarians assume and assert the desired conclusion without showing proof that substantiates it!

(2) Hebrews 4:1-11 says: **"Let us therefore fear, lest, a promise being left us of entering into his rest, any of you should seem to come short of it.**

For unto us was the gospel preached, as well as unto them; but the word preached did not profit them, not being mixed with faith in them that heard it.

For we which have believed do enter into rest, as he said, As I have sworn in my wrath, if they shall enter into my rest: although the works were finished from the foundation of the world.

For he spake in a certain place of the seventh day on this wise, And God did rest the seventh day from all his works.

And in this place again, If they shall enter into my rest.

Seeing therefore it remaineth that some must enter therein, and they to whom it was first preached entered not in because of unbelief:

Again, he limiteth a certain day, saying in David, Today, after so long a time; as it is said, Today if ye will hear his voice, harden not your hearts.

For if Jesus ["Joshua" acc. to footnote-ed] **had given them rest, then would he not afterward have spoken of another day.**

There remaineth therefore a rest to the people of God. For he that is entered into his rest, he also hath ceased from his own works, as God did from his.

Let us labour therefore to enter into that rest, lest any man fall after the same example of unbelief." NOTE: In the above verses we have the context of the statement made in verse 9.

(3) Please observe that the text (4:9) says **"a rest"** remains to the people of God. It does not say **"the sabbath"**

is to be kept holy by the people of God. A vast difference in the two statements! You can see it, can't you?

(4) The ASV says **"a sabbath rest"** remains for the people of God. It does not say "the sabbath rest" *is to be kept holy by the people of God*! A vast difference in the two statements!

(5) According to The New STRONG'S Exhaustive Concordance of the Bible, the word *sabbath* in the New Testament (KJV) always comes from *sabbaton* whereas the word *rest* in Heb. 4:9 comes from *sabbatismos* and it appears only this one time! It is a different word. According to STRONG'S GREEK DICTIONARY the word *sabbatismos* is from a der. of *sabbaton*. NOTE: *Sabbatismos* is not from *sabbaton* but is from a derivative of *sabbaton*. They are different words. *Sabbaton* is neuter gender whereas *sabbatismos* masculine gender!

(6) We learn from Heb. 3:7-19 that the Israelites failed to enter into God's rest because of their unbelief. The rest they failed to enter into was the promised land, Canaan. NOTE: They were keeping the sabbath day holy but they did not enter into God's rest. It necessarily follows that God's rest in these verses is not the keeping of the seventh day sabbath although God did rest on the seventh day!

(7) Verse 11 says, **"Let us labour therefore to enter into that rest, lest any man fall after the same example of unbelief."** The rest that remains for the people of God is something that we can fail to enter. NOTE: In this context this could not have reference to the keeping the seventh day sabbath holy because one does not have to fear and labour in order to keep the sabbath holy! One had to cease from working in order to keep the seventh day sabbath.

48

(8) If the Hebrew Christians were keeping the sabbath day holy as Sabbatarians contend, that is proof sufficient to show that **"a rest"** that remains for the people of God is *not* remembering the sabbath day and keeping it holy as they were.

(9) No doubt, contextually, **"a rest"** that remains to the people of God is not "the sabbath" that the children of Israel were told to "remember" and to "keep it holy." (Exodus 20:8). **"A rest"** that remains to the people of God refers to *"a day of eternal rest"*! It is not a 24-hour day! Unless we fear and labour to enter **"into his** [God's - ed] **rest"** we may fail to enter just as those Israelites failed to enter Canaan.

(10) In Rev. 14:13 we read: **"... Blessed are the dead which die in the Lord from henceforth: Yea, saith the Spirit, that they may rest from their labours; and their works do follow them."** NOTE: When a person dies in the Lord he ceases his labours and enters into a period of rest.

No, Heb. 4:9 does not prove that Christians should keep the sabbath day holy as the Israelites did. However, in its context it does teach that there is **"a rest"** that remains for the people of God!

22. "THE PROPHET ISAIAH PROPHESIED (42:21) THAT CHRIST WOULD 'MAGNIFY THE LAW, AND MAKE IT HONOURABLE.' "
REPLY:

(1) The Sabbatarian who makes the above argument assumes and asserts his desired conclusion without proving his conclusion from the text! The conclusion he draws is that the law refers to the sabbath

command and therefore Christians are obligated to keep the sabbath day holy! Of course, this conclusion does not necessarily follow. It is an assumption and an assertion without proof. Sabbatarians are "assumers" and "asserters"!

(2) Isaiah 42:21 says: **"The Lord is well pleased for his righteousness' sake; he will magnify the law, and make it honourable."** NOTE: This may or may not be a prophecy concerning Jesus Christ. Assuming that it is, let us consider the following. It is a fact that the text does not specifically mention either the sabbath command or Christians.

(3) The text does say that **"...He will magnify the law, and make it honourable."** However, the text does *not* say **"He will magnify the** *sabbath* **law and make it honourable!"** The text simply says **"the law."** Sabbatarians are quick to assume and assert that it is the *sabbath* law! Proof would be more in order! The text is simply saying that the Lord would magnify the law. He would respect and obey the law and encourage others to do likewise. He would do nothing to dishonour or desecrate the law.

(4) Jesus Christ **"was made under the law, To redeem them that were under the law, that we might receive the adoption of sons"**. (Gal. 4:4-5). He did not violate he *Old Covenant*. He did not transgress God's law. He kept the law! He always pleased the Father! No one could convict (convince) Jesus of sin! He was tempted, but He did not sin! (Cf. I John 3:3; John 8:29; 8:46; Heb. 4:15; 1 Peter 2:21-24). Yes, Jesus magnified the law (not merely a part of the law, but the law) and made it honourable in His own life and taught others to respect it in their own lives.

(5) The fact that Christ would magnify the law does not prove that Christians should keep the sabbath day

50

holy any more than it proves that Christians should observe the Passover, practice circumcision, etc. QUESTION: Is "the law" binding on Christians today? Of course not!

23. "PSALMS 111:7-8 SAYS '...ALL HIS COMMANDMENTS ARE SURE. THEY STAND FAST FOREVER AND EVER, AND ARE DONE IN TRUTH AND UPRIGHTNESS.' THIS INCLUDES THE COMMAND-MENT TO KEEP THE SABBATH DAY HOLY."
REPLY:

(1) This passage does not specifically mention the sabbath command. Neither does it mention any other specific commandment. The sabbath command is not suggested by either the text or the context any more than any other commandment of the Lord!

(2) The text says **"all his commandments are sure"** and **"stand fast forever and ever."** Does this mean that all the commandments God ever gave anyone at anytime for any reason are binding on Christians today?

What about the command that God gave Noah to *build an ark* in Gen.6:14 or to Abraham to *offer Isaac* in Gen. 22:2 or to Moses to *speak to the rock* in Numbers 20:1-12 or to Samuel to *utterly destroy all* the Amalekites in 1 Sam. 15:3 or to Joshua (& soldiers)to *compass the city of Jericho thirteen times* in Joshua 6 or to the apostles to *tarry in Jerusalem till they were endued with power from on* high in Luke 24:49? Were any of these commandments unsure? Did they fail to stand steadfast? Of course not. Since they are sure and stand fast are they binding on Christians? No! Neither is the sabbath command that God gave to Israel binding on Christians today!

The fact that all God's commandments are sure and

stand fast forever and ever and are done in truth and uprightness does not mean that they all are binding on Christians. All that God gave to Christians are binding on them!

24. "JESUS TAUGHT THE OBSERVANCE OF THE SABBATH DAY, BUT HE NEVER TAUGHT ANYONE TO KEEP THE OLD SACRIFICES OF THE LAW OF MOSES."
REPLY:

(1) The above argument is intended to make uninformed readers think that there were two distinct laws given to govern the Israelites. It is claimed that one law contained the ten commandments and the other law contained burning of incense, burnt offerings, sacrifices, feast days, circumcision, etc. It is further alleged that Jesus bound the ten commandment law on Christians, but he did not teach anyone to keep the law that contained the animal sacrifices, burnt offerings, etc. They claim that it was the one that was nailed to the cross. NOTE: This distinction is claimed, but the facts do not support it.

(2) The above argument assumes and asserts that Jesus never taught anyone to keep the sacrifices of the law of Moses. However, this statement is not true. The truth is that Jesus did teach others to observe the law that required sacrifices, etc. In Mark 1:44 Jesus said to the leper whom He had healed: **"See thou say nothing to any man: but go thy way, shew thyself to the priest, and offer for thy cleansing those things which Moses commanded, for a testimony unto them."** (Cf. Luke 5:14; Lev. 14). Sacrifices as required by the law of the Lord were made for Jesus according to Luke 2:21-24. Jesus taught His disciples and others saying: **"The**

52

scribes Pharisees sit in Moses' seat: All therefore whatsoever they bid you observe, that observe and do..." (Mt. 22:2-3).

QUESTION: Does the fact that Jesus taught His disciples and others to observe the teachings of the Law of Moses prove that the law of Moses is binding on Christians? Of course not! OBSERVATION: The fact that Jesus kept the sabbath and taught others to do so does not prove that the keeping of the sabbath is binding on Christians!

(3) The fact that Jesus taught others to offer sacrifices, etc. according to the Law of the Lord does not prove that the offering of sacrifices as required by the law is binding on Christians today! However, it is a fact that Jesus did teach others to offer sacrifices as required by the law! Those who say otherwise are simply wrong!

No, the sabbath law is *not* binding on Christians!

25. "IN THE NEW TESTAMENT WHEN WE ARE TOLD TO KEEP OR OBEY THE LAW OF GOD (OR GOD'S COMMANDMENTS) IT ALWAYS MEANS OR INCLUDES THE SABBATH COMMAND."
   REPLY:

(1) The Sabbatarian who makes the above argument assumes and asserts his desired conclusion without proving his conclusion from the text!

(2) The only way that one could know that the command to keep the sabbath is included would be by the text or immediate context or the general context of the Scriptures indicating that such is the case. Assuming and asserting that the sabbath command is always (or even one time) included does not prove that such is the case. Sabbatarians are obligated to prove the sabbath command is meant.

53

(3) Here are some questions for Sabbatarians: *"Did God ever have any commandments beside the ten com-mandments? If so, what were they? Does He now have any commandments beside the ten? If so, what are they?"* OBSERVATION: If God has some commandments (or a law), besides the ten commandments how would a Sabbatarian know that the expression **"the law"** or **"commandments"** always includes the sabbath command. The truth is they don't! Another question is: *"Have any of God's commandments been discontinued? If not, should we keep every commandment that God ever gave anyone? If yes, is it possible that the command given to the Israelites to keep the sabbath day holy has been discontinued and does not apply to anyone today?"*

(4) God gave Adam a command not to eat of the fruit of the tree of knowledge of good and evil which was in the midst of the Garden of Eden. (Cf. Gen. 2:15-17; 3:1-3). NOTE: This was not one of the ten commandments. God gave Noah some commands relative to building the ark, going into the ark, etc. (Cf. Gen. 6:14-22; 7:1-5, 9, 16; Heb. 11:7.) NOTE: This was not one of the ten commandments. God gave Abraham a number of commandments and he kept them according to Gen. 26:5. (Also cf. Gen. 12:1-4; 17:9-14; 22:1-19; Heb. 11:8, 17; James 2:21-23). NOTE: The command to keep the sabbath day was not included in any of these commandments.

PROOF: There is nothing in any of the texts or contexts to indicate that any of the commandments mentioned above included the command to keep the sabbath day holy. In addition to this we read the following in Nehemiah 9:13-14: **"Thou camest down also upon mount Sinai, and spakest with them from heaven, and gavest them**

54

right judgments, and true laws, good statutes and commandments; And madest known unto them thy holy sabbath, and commandedst them, precepts, statutes, and laws, by the hand of Moses thy servant: And gavest them bread from heaven..." NOTE: The sabbath was made known to the Israelites beginning in Exodus 16. There is no Scriptural proof that any man was ever commanded to keep the sabbath day holy before it was given to the Israelites.

(5) There is absolutely no proof that such passages as 1 Cor. 7:19; 1 John 2:3; 3:4; 3:24; 5:3; Rev. 12:17; 14:12; 22:14 refer to the ten commandments which includes the command to keep the sabbath day holy!

(6) In writing to the church at Corinth the apostle Paul said: **"If any man think himself to be a prophet, or spiritual, let him acknowledge that the things that I write unto you are the commandments of the Lord."** (1 Cor. 14:37).

NOTE: There is no evidence that Paul ever taught (either by letter or orally) that the saints at Corinth (or Christians anywhere) should keep the sabbath day holy as the Israelites (including himself) under the first covenant were taught to do.

In 1 Cor. 5 God commanded (through Paul) the saints to put away from among them the brother that was a fornicator. He told them not to keep company with **"any man that is called a brother"** who is **"a fornicator, or covetous, or an idolater, or a railer, or a drunkard, or an extortioner"**. He said: **"with such an one no not to eat."** In 7:10-11 the Lord gave this command: **"Let not the wife depart from her husband..."**

In 10:31 He said: **"...Do all to the glory of God."** In 11:23-34 the Lord gave some commands relative to the Lord's Supper. In 1 Cor. 14:34-35 Paul said: **"Let your women keep silence in the churches..."** In 1 Cor. 16:2 he said:

55

"Upon the first day of the week let every one of you lay by him in store, as God hath prospered him,..."

NOTE: The above things in 1 Corinthians are some commandments of the Lord. There are many other commandments that the Lord gave in the New Testament that were not given in the Old Testament.

OBSERVATION: The Lord never commanded any Christian to keep the sabbath day holy!

CHALLENGE: We sincerely challenge Sabbatarians to produce a passage of Scripture that shows that God commands Christians to keep the sabbath day holy!

26. "JESUS TOLD THE RICH YOUNG RULER TO KEEP THE TEN COMMANDMENTS WHICH INCLUDED THE SABBATH COMMAND. HE SAID: **'IF THOU WILT ENTER INTO LIFE, KEEP THE COMMANDMENTS.'** (MT. 19:17)."
REPLY:

(1) The Sabbatarian who makes the above argument assumes and asserts his desired conclusion without proving his conclusion from the text! The conclusion he wants us to draw is that since Jesus (during His life here on earth) told someone to keep the sabbath at that time proves that therefore Christians are obligated to keep the sabbath day holy! Of course, this conclusion does not necessarily follow; it is an assumption and an assertion without proof.

(2) A reading of Mt. 19:16-22; Mk. 10:17-22 and Luke 18:18-23 will give additional information regarding Jesus and the ruler on the occasion under consideration.

(3) It is obvious that Jesus did tell the rich young ruler to **"keep the commandments"** which included the sabbath command. However, this does not teach that

Christians should keep the sabbath day holy. NOTE: The fact that Jesus told the cleansed leper to go show himself to the priest **"and offer for thy cleansing those things which Moses commanded, for a testimony unto them,"** (Mk. 1:44), does not prove that we should go to a priest and offer the things that Moses commanded in Lev. 14:1-32. (Please read that passage and see what the cleansed leper had to do because He commanded him to keep the law under which he then lived.)

Jesus kept the law under which He lived and taught others to keep that law, but He did not keep that Old Testament law nor did He teach others to do so *after His Testament* (the New Testament*) came into effect after His death*, resurrection and *ascension into heaven.* (Cf. Heb. 7:12; 7:19; 8:6-13; 9:16-17; 12:24; 13:20; 2 Cor. 3:6).

The fact that Jesus was circumcised or kept the sabbath does not prove or even suggest that Christians must be circumcised or keep the sabbath!

(4) Yes, Jesus told the rich young ruler that if he would have eternal life he would have to keep the commandments (which included the sabbath command) because he was then living under the law that God gave to Israel through Moses! However, Christians are not told to keep the sabbath holy because they are not living under that law that God gave to Israel through Moses!

27."GOD SAID: 'REMEMBER THE SABBATH DAY, TO KEEP IT HOLY' (EXO. 20:8). THE WORD *REMEMBER* PROVES THAT GOD HAD PRE-VIOUSLY GIVEN THE SABBATH AND THEY HAD ALREADY BEEN OBSERVING IT BEFORE LEAVING EGYPT. OTHERWISE GOD WOULD NOT HAVE SAID

57

TO REMEMBER IT."
REPLY:
(1) Even if the above argument were true, this would not prove that Christians should keep the sabbath day holy. It would only mean that God had made known the sabbath to the Israelites prior to the giving of the law at Sinai. However, this would conflict with the truth stated in Nehemiah 9:13-14 that teaches that God came down on Mt. Sinai and made known to the Israelites the sabbath and gave them other commandments, laws, precepts, etc.

(2) The word *remember* does not necessarily mean that you knew something prior to being told to remember it or that the event you are told to remember had occurred sometime previous to that occasion. For example, on one's wedding day I may say to the bride and groom, *"Remember the wedding day, to celebrate it each year."* This does not mean that there had been a previous wedding for them and they were to remember it.

Remember means to be mindful of or to keep in memory or to bring to mind.

No, there is no proof that the Israelites kept the sabbath day holy prior to their leaving Egypt.

Pure unfounded assertion
28. "NOT ONLY DID THE NATION OF ISRAEL HAVE THE TEN COMMANDMENT LAW BUT ALL NATIONS HAD IT. WHEN THEY FAILED TO KEEP THE SABBATH DAY HOLY THEY WERE PUNISHED."
REPLY:
(1) There is no proof that God ever commanded the heathen nations of the world to keep the sabbath day holy.

58

(2) Even if the above statements were true, this would *not* prove that Christians are obligated to keep the sabbath day holy.

(3) The above statements are not true! Here is proof. Speaking to Israel, God said: **"For what nation is there so great, who hath God so nigh unto them, as the Lord our God is in all things that we call upon him for? And what nation is there so great, that hath statutes and judgments so righteous as all this law, which I set before you this day?"** (Deut. 4:7-8). NOTE: This settles it! No other nation had **"statutes and judgments so righteous as all this law"** which certainly included the sabbath law.

FURTHER NOTE: The sabbath law was given to the nation of Israel because the Israelites had been servants in Egypt and God led them out of bondage. (Cf. Deut. 5:15).

29. "IF NINE OF THE TEN COMMANDMENTS (ALL EXCEPT THE COMMAND TO KEEP THE SABBATH) ARE INCLUDED IN THE NEW COVENANT, THEN THE NEW COVENANT IS ACCORDING TO THE OLD COVENANT. BUT THE LORD PLAINLY SAYS THE NEW COVENANT WOULD NOT BE ACCORDING TO THE OLD COVENANT."

REPLY:

(1) It is true that the New Testament (Covenant) forbids idolatry, making graven images, taking God's name in vain, murder, adultery, stealing, bearing false witness against our neighbors and coveting their things. It also requires us to honor our parents. But it is also true that it goes far beyond these things in its prohibitions and requirements. Here are some examples:

A. It not only prohibits killing, but it also

prohibits being angry with a brother without a cause. (See Mt. 5:21-22).

B. It not only prohibits adultery, but it also prohibits lusting after a woman. (See Mt. 5:27-28).

Although there are some things in the New Testament that were in the Old, it is truly a *New* Covenant! It is *not according to the Covenant that God made with Israel when He led them out of Egypt.*

(2) In view of the above argument, please observe the fact that Sabbatarians (according to the above argument) would have the New Covenant exactly like the Old Covenant because they include all ten commandments (including the sabbath command) in the New Covenant! NOTE: Of course, we recognize the fact that there were many other prohibitions, requirements and regulations in the Old Covenant besides the ten commandments!

(3) Even if the above argument were true this would not prove that Christians should keep the sabbath day holy as did the Israelites under the Old Covenant. Christians are under **"a better covenant, which was established upon better promises"** and it (the *New* Testament) does *not* command Christians to keep the sabbath day holy! (See Heb. 8:6).

30. "ACCORDING TO JER. 31:31-34 & HEBREWS 8:8-13 THE DIFFERENCE BETWEEN THE OLD COVENANT AND THE NEW COVENANT IS THAT THE OLD WAS WRITTEN ON TABLES OF STONE, BUT THE NEW WOULD BE WRITTEN IN THEIR HEARTS. IN BOTH INSTANCES IT WAS THE SAME LAW."

REPLY:

(1) It is true that God (speaking of the New Covenant) said, **"...I will put my laws into their mind, and write them in their hearts..."** (Heb. 8:10), but God did not say that this would be the only difference.

(2) God did not say that in both instances it would be the same law! In fact God said that the New Covenant *would not be* according to (or like) the one that He made with them when He led them out of Egypt.

(3) Although it is true that God puts His laws in our minds and writes them in our hearts it is also true that the laws of God have been written in what we call the Books of the New Testament. In Eph. 3:2-6 Paul mentions the fact that God revealed the gospel, (the faith , the law of liberty), to him and he wrote it down so others could read and understand what he knew. (Also see John 20:30-31; 1 Cor. 4:6; Rev. 22:18-19; 1 John 5:13; Col. 4:6; 1 Thess. 5:27; 2 Thess. 2:15; 2 Thess. 3:14; 2 Peter 3:1, 16; Acts 15:19-32; 1 Cor. 14:37, etc.)

(4) The Hebrew writer says: **"For the priesthood being changed, there is made of necessity a change also of the law."** (7:12). It was essential that the law be changed in view of the change in the priesthood.

(5) The above argument falls far short of proving that the sabbath law is still in effect! No, the New Covenant *is not* according to the Old Covenant!

31. "THE AGREEMENT THAT THE ISRAELITES MADE IN EXO. 19 TO DO ALL THAT THE LORD HAD SPOKEN WAS THE COVENANT THAT WAS DONE AWAY, NOT THE TEN COMMANDMENTS."
REPLY:

(1) It is true that the Israelites broke their agreement to do all that God had spoken. However, their agreement was not the covenant that was done away. Please note the fact that God said, "**...If ye will obey my voice indeed, and keep my covenant...**" (Exo. 19:5). God did not say, "If you will keep your agreement...", but He said, "**...my covenant...**"

(2) Consider also the fact that God (speaking of the *covenant* and the Israelites) said, "**...which *my* covenant they brake...**" (Jer. 31:32). God did not say, *"which their agreement they brake"* but "***my* covenant they brake**"! A big difference! See the difference?

(3) It was the covenant that they broke that was done away according to Hebrews 8:7-13. God did not do away with the agreement that Israel made. The Israelites did not keep their agreement and thus they did away with it!

(4) In Deut. 9:11 Moses identifies the "**two tables of stone**" as the "**tables of the covenant**". In Deut. 4:13 we learn that God declared unto Israel "**his covenant**" that he commanded Israel to perform, "**even the ten commandments**" which He wrote upon two tables of stone. It was *God's Covenant*, not their agreement!

32. "ISAIAH 66:22-23 TEACHES THAT THE SABBATH WILL BE OBSERVED IN THE NEW HEAVEN AND THE NEW EARTH. IN VIEW OF THIS, CHRISTIANS SHOULD BE KEEPING THE SABBATH DAY HOLY."
REPLY:
(1) The desired conclusion is assumed and asserted, but not proven! False positions require assumptions.

(2) The fact that a thing may be done in the next age does not necessarily prove that it is binding on Christ-ians in this age!

(3) *If* (and that's a big *"if"*) Isaiah 66:22-23 teaches what Sabbatarians claim, then that would simply prove that in another age the sabbath would be observed. That would *not prove* that Christians *in this age* must keep the sabbath day holy in order to please God.

(4) If Isaiah 66:22-23 binds *"sabbath keeping"* on Christians in this age, it would also bind the keeping of the **"new moons"** which involved *burnt offerings*, etc. (Cf. 1 Chron. 23:31; 2 Chron. 2:4; 8:13; 31:3; Ezra 3:5; Neh. 10:33; etc.). NOTE: This would reinstate (or re-institute) the old system of the Israelites, which is inferior to the system of faith revealed in the New Testament of Jesus Christ, to be followed in the next age. I don't believe that most Sabbatarians will accept that. Are you willing to?

(5) We know that Christians will not be condemned for not keeping the sabbath, the new moon, etc. because Paul said: **"Let no man therefore judge you in meat, or in drink, or in respect of an holy day, or of the new moon, or of the sabbath days: Which are a shadow of things to come; but the body is of Christ."** (Col. 2:16-17).

No, Isaiah 66:22-23 *does not prove* that the sabbath law of the Old testament is binding on Christians!

33. "IN ACTS 15:21 JAMES SAID: 'FOR MOSES OF OLD TIME HATH IN EVERY CITY THEM THAT PREACH HIM, BEING READ IN THE SYNAGOGUES EVERY SABBATH DAY.' THIS PROVES THAT THE SABBATH WAS BEING KEPT ABOUT 20 YEARS AFTER THE RESURRECTION OF CHRIST."

63

REPLY:

(1) The desired conclusion of the Sabbatarian is that Christians must keep the sabbath day holy because James mentioned the sabbath about 20 years after the resurrection of Christ. To reach that conclusion one must make assumptions and assertions that are not warranted.

(2) In Acts 15:21 James did *not* have reference to Christians when he said **"... Moses... hath in every city them that preach him, being read in the synagogues every sabbath day."** Christians did not preach Moses nor read Moses in the synagogues every sabbath day! They preached Christ! The synagogues were places where the Jews met to preach and read Moses every sabbath day. When Paul wrote 2 Corinthians 3:15 he said: **"But even unto this day, when Moses is read, the veil is upon their heart."**

NOTE: Those who preached Moses in the synagogues every sabbath were Israelites, who because of the veil upon their heart, did not understand that the law that God gave through Moses to Israel at Mt. Sinai had been abrogated at the cross. This included the ten commandments. (Cf. Col. 2:14-17; Rom. 7:1-7; Heb. 8:6-13; 7:12, 19; 10:9; Gal. 5:4; etc.) The same is true of Sabbatarians today. They have **"the veil upon their heart."** We are praying for its removal.

(3) When Paul (as an apostle of Christ) went into the synagogues on the sabbath days **"and reasoned with them out of the scriptures"** he was *not* preaching Moses, but he was preaching Christ! (Cf. Acts 17:1-3).

No, the statement of James in Acts 15:21 does not prove that the sabbath law is binding on Christians!

34. "GOD COMMANDED THE ISRAELITES TO KEEP THE SABBATH DAY HOLY. SINCE GOD IS NO RESPECTOR OF PERSONS AS TAUGHT IN ACTS

10:34; ROM. 2:11 AND EPH. 6:9, CHRISTIANS TODAY MUST ALSO KEEP THE SABBATH DAY HOLY."
   REPLY:
   (1) It is true that God commanded the Israelites to remember the sabbath day to keep it holy in such passages as Exo. 20:1-17; Deut. 5:1-22; etc. It is also true that the New Testament teaches that God is no respector of persons (in the above and other passages). However, it is *not* true that Christians must keep the sabbath day holy as the Israelites were required to do.

   (2) The fact that God commanded Noah to build an ark (Cf. Gen. 6:22) does not mean that all other people (including Christians) are obligated to build arks. The fact that God commanded Abraham (and the Israelites) to practice circumcision (Cf. Gen. 17:9-14; Lev. 12:1-3) does not make it obligatory that Christians practice circumcision. The fact that God commanded the Israelites to offer burnt offerings, animal sacrifices, etc. does not prove that Christians must offer these things today!

   35. THE TEN COMMANDMENTS CONSTI-TUTE THE COMPLETE RELATIONSHIP BETWEEN MAN AND MAN, AND MAN AND GOD."
   REPLY:
   (1) Obviously, the above statement is made in an effort to get people to believe that Christians today should keep the sabbath day holy. Even if the argument were true in the dispensation covered by the Old Covenant, it would not necessarily prove that Christians under the New Covenant would be bound to keep the sabbath holy. Christians have never been under the Old Covenant. We are under law to Christ. (Cf. 1 Cor. 9:21). We are under the New Covenant (or Testament) of Jesus Christ! (Cf. Heb. 1:1-2;

Heb. 2:1-4; 7:12; 7:19, 22; 8:6-13; 9:15-17; 10:9-10).

(2) I have read and heard the above statement made a number of times through the years. However, I have never read nor heard any evidence given that proves that such is the case. Assumptions and allegations are easily made, but stating such does not prove the truthfulness of the statement. Where is the *Scriptural proof?*

(3) If "the ten commandments constitute the complete relationship between man and man, and man and God," that means it covers the whole thing, doesn't it? Let me ask some questions. Is it wrong (sinful) for a man to bear false witness *for* his neighbor? Is it wrong (sinful) for a man to bear false witness *against* his enemy? NOTE: If your answer is yes, please show which of the ten commandments are violated when a man does either of these things.

(4) When Sabbatarians claim that the ten commandments constitute the complete relationship between man and man, and man and God they are including the idea that the ten commandments are a perfect moral code.

I have never fully understood how hundreds of thousands of people can be "taken in" and deceived by mere assumptions and allegations. *Proof* is never given because there is no proof to substantiate the claim that the ten commandments are a perfect moral code. Neither is there any *proof* to substantiate the claim that the ten commandments constitute the complete relationship between man and man, and man and God.

Are the ten commandments a perfect moral code and a complete relationship between man and man, and man and God? Where is the *Scriptural proof?*

66

(5) The New Testament forbids or condemns a brother going to law against a brother before unbelievers. (See 1 Cor. 6:1-8). In other words, a Christian has no right to sue another Christian in the courts of the land. It is wrong for Christians to sue other Christians in the courts of the world. QUESTION: Which one of the ten commandments forbids or condemns a brother for going to law against another? ANSWER: Not a single one! However, it is God's will that such be forbidden and condemned! The ten commandments fall short here, don't they? A perfect law?

(6) The New Testament forbids or condemns divorce, i.e., the putting away of one's spouse and marrying another (except it be for fornication) in Mark 10:11-12; Luke 16:18; Matthew 5:31-32 and 19:9. In other words, *it is sinful for a person to divorce his/her spouse* (except it be for fornication) *and marry another.* Other passages forbid or condemn divorce even if a person does not marry another. (Cf. Matthew 19:4-8; Rom. 7:2-3; 1 Cor. 7:2-5; 7:10-11; 7:39; Eph. 5:22-33). QUESTION: Which one of the ten commandments forbids or condemns divorce as stated above? ANSWER: Not a single one! However, it is God's will that such be forbidden and condemned! The ten commandments fall short here, don't they? A perfect moral code? Of course not! Again Sabbatarians make a false claim.

(7) The New Testament forbids or condemns drunkenness in such passages as Eph. 5:18; Romans 13:13; 1 Cor. 5:11; 6:9-11 and Gal. 5:19-21. QUESTION: Which one of the ten commandments forbids or condemns drunkenness? ANSWER: Not a single one! A person can obey every one of the ten commandments and still be a drunkard! Such a person shall not inherit the kingdom of God! NOTE: The ten commandments are not a perfect moral code and do not

67

constitute a complete relationship between man and man, and man and God!

(8) The New Testament forbids or condemns murmuring (complaining, grumbling) in such passages as James 5:9; 1 Cor. 10:10 and Phil. 2:14. Obviously, it is sinful for a person to murmur. QUESTION: Which one of the ten commandments prohibits or condemns murmuring? The answer is simple. Not a one!

(9) The New Testament prohibits or condemns dishonoring the king. Peter said: **"...Honour the king."** (1 Peter 2:17). The apostle Paul teaches us in Rom. 13:1-7 to be subject to civil powers and to pay tribute. He says: **"Render therefore to all their dues: tribute to whom tribute is due; custom to whom custom; fear to whom fear; honour to whom honour."** NOTE: Since we are taught to honour the rulers we can certainly see that dishonoring the king is prohibited or condemned. QUESTION: Where do any of the ten commandments prohibit or condemn dishonoring civil rulers? The answer is clear. No where!

(10) The New Testament prohibits or condemns hypocrisy in such passages as Romans 12:9 and 1 Peter 2:1-2. During His personal ministry here on earth Jesus Christ repeatedly condemned the scribes and Pharisees became of their hypocrisy. He called them *"hypocrites"* in such passages as Matthew 23 and Luke 11:44. QUESTION: Which one of the ten commandments prohibits or condemns hypocrisy as such? Not a single one! Does this sound like the ten commandments are a complete relationship between man and man, and man and God? A perfect moral code? *Of course not!*

When we examine by the *Scriptures* the claims of Sabbatarians relative to the ten commandments being a complete relationship between man and man, and man and God, they fail the *Scriptural test*! No, *the ten commandments are not a perfect moral code!*

36. "JAMES 2:10 (WHICH SAYS, 'FOR WHO-SOEVER SHALL KEEP THE WHOLE LAW, AND YET OFFEND IN ONE POINT, HE IS GUILTY OF ALL') REFERS TO THE SABBATH LAW BECAUSE IN VERSE 11 JAMES QUOTES TWO OF THE TEN COMMANDMENTS."
REPLY:

(1) Assuming and asserting that a thing is so does not prove it to be so.

(2) Does the fact that James (in the context in verse 11) quoted two of the commandments that are contained in the ten commandments prove that James was binding the ten commandments on Christians in verse 10? Of course not!

(3) If the fact that James quoted two of the commandments that are contained in the ten commandments proves that he was binding all of the ten commandments on Christians, then it would also prove that since in verse 8 (in the same context) James quoted one of the commandments that are contained in what Sabbatarians call "the law of Moses" (or "the ceremonial law"), that he was binding *all* of the commandments contained in "the law of Moses"! NOTE: In verse 8 James said: **"If ye fulfill the royal law according to the Scripture, Thou shalt love thy neighbor as thyself, ye do well."** This commandment *is not* one of the ten commandments. It is found in Lev. 19:18.

Are Sabbatarians ready to accept the obvious conclusion of their reasoning? Are they ready to bind *all* of of *"the law of Moses"* on Christians? NOTE: That which proves too much proves nothing!

(4) Please observe the fact that James did *not* quote the command to keep the sabbath! In fact, no apostle ever commanded any Christian to keep the sabbath day holy!

(5) Contextually, *"the whole law"* that James mentions in verse 10 seems to be **"the royal law"** of verse 8. This same law is spoken of in verse 12 as **"the law of liberty"** by which we shall be judged. No doubt, James referred to the same law in James 1:25 when he said: **"But whoso looketh into the perfect law of liberty, and continueth therein, he being not a forgetful hearer, but a doer of the work, this man shall be blessed in his deed."** NOTE: The law of Moses did not liberate. It was a law of sin and death!

(6) No, James 2:10 does *not* refer to the sabbath law! It was not a **"perfect law of liberty"** as we have seen.

37. "THE FACT THAT THE SABBATH IS MENTIONED A NUMBER OF TIMES AFTER THE CROSS PROVES THAT THE SABBATH IS TO BE OBSERVED BY CHRISTIANS."
REPLY:
(1) This argument is merely an assumption and an assertion! The fact that a thing is mentioned in the New Testament after the cross *does not prove* that it is binding upon Christians.

(2) Pentecost, sacrifices (animal) and burnt offerings are mentioned after the cross. Does that prove that Christians should observe Pentecost, offer animal sacrifices and burnt offerings?

(3) Circumcision is mentioned four or five times

as much as the sabbath is after the cross. Does this prove that physical circumcision is bound on Christians? Of course not! (Cf. Gal. 5:1-6).

38. "JAMES 1:25 REFERS TO THE TEN COMMANDMENTS WHEN IT SAYS, 'BUT WHO LOOKETH INTO THE PERFECT LAW OF LIBERTY, AND CONTINUETH THEREIN, HE BEING NOT A FORGETFUL HEARER, BUT A DOER OF THE WORK, THIS MAN SHALL BE BLESSED IN HIS DEED.' THEREFORE, THE TEN COMMANDMENT LAW IS THE PERFECT LAW OF LIBERTY."
REPLY:
(1) Again we see Sabbatarians assuming and asserting things without *Scriptural proof.*

(2) The law that contained the ten commandments was given to a nation (the nation of Israel) that God had delivered from Egyptian bondage. (See Exodus 20:1-17; Deuteronomy 5:1-21, etc.). *It was not given to any other nation.* He did *not* deliver any other nation from bondage in Egypt. So the law that contained the ten commandments was limited in scope. It applied only to those of the nation of Israel and those who became Jewish proselytes. Please note the fact that *"the perfect law of liberty"* is of universal application. James said, **"But *whoso* looketh into the perfect law of liberty and continueth therein..."** NOTE: In view of this we can see that the *"ten commandment law"* is not the *"perfect law of liberty"*.

(3). James 1:25 *does not refer* to the law that contained the ten commandments because Hebrews 7:19 says: **"For the law made nothing perfect, but the bringing in of a better hope did; by the which we draw nigh unto God."** NOTE: The law (which contained the ten commandments)

71

made nothing perfect, but the law of James 1:25 is a **"perfect law"** that liberates!

The **"perfect law of liberty"** of James 1:25 is the same **"law of liberty"** of James 2:12 by which we shall be judged! NOTE: According to Romans 2:16 we will be judged by Jesus Christ according to the **"gospel"** that Paul preached.

We learn from John 12:48 that the words of Christ will judge us in the last day. In view of this verse and Romans 2:16 and James 2:12 the words of Christ, the gospel and the law of liberty must be one and the same thing. They are different expressions referring to the same thing. NOTE: These expressions *do not refer* to the ten commandment law!

39. "CHRISTIANS SHOULD KEEP THE SAB-BATH BECAUSE GOD SAID, 'I CHANGE NOT' AND JESUS CHRIST IS 'THE SAME YESTERDAY, TODAY AND FOREVER' (Mal. 3:6; Heb. 13:8)."
   REPLY:
   (1) The fact that God does not change and Jesus Christ is the same yesterday, today and forever *does not* prove that the sabbath law is binding on Christians. It *does* prove that God *Himself* does not change and that *Jesus Christ* remains the same, in some sense.

   (2) Does the fact that God does not change and Jesus remains the same prove that circumcision, animal sacrifices, burnt offerings, burning incense, etc. are binding on Christians since they were bound on the Israelites? If not, then how does the fact that God does not change and Jesus remains the same prove that sabbath keeping is binding on Christians?

(3) Does the fact that God does not change and remains the same prove that inflicting the death the penalty for sabbath violation (see Exo. 35:1-2) is binding on Christians since it was bound on the Israelites? *Of course not!* Neither does it prove that the sabbath is bound on Christians!

AS WE CONTINUE OUR EXAMINATION OF SAB-BATARIANISM, PLEASE CONSIDER THE FOLLOWING

I. If the commandment to **"Remember the sabbath day, to keep it holy"** (Exo. 20:8) is a moral commandment and is binding on people today, then all people who do not keep the sabbath are immoral! NOTE: Do Sabbatarians consider all non-sabbath keepers as immoral? Do they? To be consistent they must do so! Do they tell all their friends that?

II. In Exo. 35:2 the **sabbath** is spoken of as **"an holy day"**. Other things such as the **tabernacle, vessels in the tabernacle, perfume, anointing oil** and **the firstling of a cow, sheep or a goat** are spoken of as being **"holy"**. Cf. Exo. 40:9; Kings 8:4; Exo. 30:34-37; 30:25 & Num. 18:17). However, a number of things (such as **the tabernacle, ark of the testimony, tables** and **vessels, candlestick** and **vessels, altar of incense, altar of burnt offerings** and **vessels, the place where the sin offering was killed, the altar, the atonement** and **part of the tabernacle** are spoken of as being *"most holy"*! (Cf. Exo. 30:25-30; Lev. 6:25; Exo. 29:37; 30:10 & Exo. 26:33). Please observe the fact that the sabbath is *not* spoken of as being *"most holy"*!

QUESTION: Does the fact that a number of things are spoken of as being *"most holy"*, but the sabbath is *not* so described prove that those things were superior to the sabbath and are to be "observed" in some way in this age? Of course not!

III. There are seven different expressions in Nehemiah 8 that refer to the law that God gave through Moses to the Israelites. They are as follows.

1. **"...The book of the law of Moses, which the Lord had commanded to Israel."** (Verse 1)

2. **"...The law..."** (Verse 2, 7, 9)

3. **"...The book of the law..."** (Verse 3)

4. **"...The book..."** (Verse 5)

5. **"...The words of the law."** (Verse 9)

6. **"...The law which the Lord had commanded by Moses..."** (Verse 14)

7. **"...The book of the law of God..."** (Verse 8, 18)

OBSERVATION: The above expressions refer to one and the same law, not to seven *different* laws.

IV. What does the expression **"the law"** embrace? It embraces the following:

1. The Book of GENESIS. In Gal. 4:21-22 Paul said: **"Tell me, ye that desire to be under the law, do ye not hear the law? For it is written, that Abraham had two sons, the one by a bondmaid, the other by a freewoman."** NOTE: We find this written in Genesis 16:15 and 21:2-3.

2. The Book of EXODUS. In Romans 7:7 Paul said: **"... For I had not known sin, but by the law: for I had not known lust, except the law had said, Thou shalt not covet."** NOTE: We find the expression, **"Thou shalt not covet"** in Exodus 20:17. Certainly **"the law"** included "Exodus".

3. The Book of LEVITICUS. Mt. 22:36-39 says that a lawyer said to Jesus, **"Master, which is the great com-**

74

mandment in the law? Jesus said unto him, **Thou shalt love the Lord thy God with all thy heart, and with all thy soul, and with all thy mind. This is the first and great commandment. And the second is like unto it, Thou shalt love thy neighbor as thyself. On these two commandments hang all the law and the prophets."** NOTE: We find **"...Thou shalt love thy neighbor as thyself"** in Leviticus 19:18. Yes, "Leviticus" is contained in **"the law"**.

4. The Book of NUMBERS. In Mt. 12:5 Jesus said: **"Or have ye not read in the law, how that on the sabbath days the priests in the temple profane the sabbath, and are blameless?"** NOTE: In Numbers 28:9-10 we find that offerings (including two lambs) would be offered on the sabbath. The priests would offer more offerings on the sabbath than any other day. When they did this they were blameless although no work was to be done on the sabbath.

5. The Book of DEUTERONOMY. In Mt. 22:36-39 Jesus quotes a commandment that is found in **"the law"** in Deuteronomy 6:5. **"The law"** included "Deuteronomy".

6. The Book of PSALMS. In John. 10:34 **"Jesus answered them, Is it not written in your law, I said, Ye are gods?"** The only other time this expression is found in the Scriptures is in Psalms 82:6. So **"the law"** included the "Psalms."

7. The Books of the PROPHETS. In 1 Cor. 14:21 Paul declared: **"In the law it is written, With men of other tongues and other lips will I speak unto this people;..."** NOTE: This is a quotation from Isaiah the prophet (28:11). So **"*the law*"** embraced "the prophets" also.

V. THE LAW OF MOSES INCLUDED MANY THINGS. Here is a list of some of the things included in **"*the law of Moses*."**

(1) *Burnt offerings*. They (the priests and others)

"builded the altar of the God of Israel, to offer burnt offerings thereon, as it is written in the law of Moses, the man of God." (Ezra 3:2). Cf. Deut. 12:5-14.

(2) *"...The fathers shall not be put to death* for the children, nor the children be put to death for the fathers; but every man shall be put to death for his own sin " according to that "which is written in the book of the law of Moses, wherein the Lord commanded..." (2 Kgs. 14:6). Referring to this, 2 Chron. 25:4 says: "the law in the book of Moses."

(3) *Josiah put away* "workers with familiar spirits, and the wizards, and the images, and the idols and all the abominations that were spied" in Jerusalem and the land of Judah "that he might perform the words of the law which were written in the book that Hilkiah the priest found in the house of the Lord." (2 Kgs. 23:24). NOTE: Verse 25 refers to it as "the law of Moses."

(4) *Purification.* "And when the days of her purification according to the law of Moses were accomplished..." (Luke 2:22).

(5) *Stone adulterers.* Speaking to Jesus of a woman they said was taken in the very act of adultery, the scribes and Pharisees said: "Now Moses in the law commanded us, that such should be stoned: but what sayest thou?" (John 8:5). Cf. Lev. 20:10; Dt. 17:6-7.

(6) *Not muzzle the ox.* The apostle Paul said: "For it is written in the law of Moses, Thou shalt not muzzle the mouth of the ox that treadeth out the corn." (1 Cor. 9:9). Cf. Deut. 25:4.

(7) *Circumcision.* Jesus said: "Moses... gave unto

76

you circumcision; (not because it is of Moses, but of the fathers;) and ye on the sabbath day circumcise a man. If a man on the sabbath day receive circumcision, that the law of Moses should not be broken; are ye angry at me, because I have made a man every whit whole on the sabbath day?" (John 7:22-23). Cf. Lev. 12:1-3.

(8) *God's ways, statutes, commandments, judgments and testimonies.* David charged Solomon to "...keep the charge of the Lord thy God, to walk in his ways, to keep his statues and his commandments, and his judgments, and his testimonies, as it is written in the law of Moses..." (1 Kgs. 2:3).

(9) *Things concerning Christ.* Jesus said: "...These are the words which I spake unto you, while I was yet with you, that all things must be fulfilled, which were written in the law of Moses, and in the prophets, and in the psalms concerning me." NOTE: In John 1:45 Philip said: "We have found him, of whom Moses in the law, and the prophets, did write, Jesus of Nazareth, the son of Joseph."

(10) *Honour thy father and thy mother.* Speaking to the Pharisees and to certain of the scribes (in Mark 7:9-10) Jesus declared: "Full well ye reject the commandment of God, that ye may keep your own tradition. For Moses said, Honour thy father and thy mother; and whoso curseth father or mother, let him die the death." (Cf. Exodus 20:12 & Deut. 5:16). NOTE: This was one of the ten commandments.

(11) *Thou shalt not kill.* Speaking to the Jews (in John 7:19-20) Jesus said: "Did not Moses give you the law, and yet none of you keepeth the law? Why go ye about to kill me? The people answered and said, Thou hast a devil: who goeth about to kill thee?" FURTHER NOTE: In John 7:19-20 Jesus taught that Moses gave the Jews the law that said,

"Thou shalt not kill" (which was one of the ten commandments) and yet they were seeking to kill him in violation of that law.

OBSERVATIONS:

A. The law of Moses not only contained such things as circumcision, purification, burnt offerings, not muzzling the ox, stoning adulterers, but also things concerning Christ, God's ways, statutes, commandments, judgments, testmonies, etc., including the ten commandments.

B. The ten commandments (as a list of commandments) are written twice in the book of the law of Moses as recorded in Exodus 20:1-17 and Deuteronomy 5:1-22.

C. The Sabbatarians are simply wrong when they make a distinction between **"the law of Moses"** which they claim was a ceremonial law and **"the law of God"** which they contend was the ten commandment law.

The truth is clear. The **"law of Moses"** contained the ten commandments as well as burnt offerings, etc. and **"the law of God (the Lord)"** contained sacrifices, etc. as well as the ten commandments.

VI. THE TEN COMMANDMENT LAW, AS SUCH, WAS A LAW OF DEATH. Sabbatarians often say, "The ten commandment law was *not* a law of death." However, this statement is never *proven* by the Scriptures. It is assumed and asserted without proof.

When a person violated most of the ten commandments he was subject to death (physical). Let us notice each of the ten commandments and see if that is so. Read Exodus

20:1-17 for a list of the ten commandments. Here they are:

(1) *No other gods* (v. 3). A reading of Deut. 13:6-11 will tell us that if a friend or a relative were to secretly say, **"Let us go and serve other gods..."** that he (or she) was to be stoned to death!

(2) *No idols or images* (v. 4-5). A reading of Deut. 13:6-18 and Exo. 22:20 indicates that a person who worships idols (which could be images) would be put to death!

(3) *Not take God's name in vain* (v. 7). A reading of Lev. 24:10-16 informs us that a person who took God's name in vain would be put to death!

(4) *Keep sabbath holy* (v. 8). We learn from Exo. 35:1-2 that death was the penalty when one violated the sabbath command by working!

(5) *Honour parents* (v. 12). A person who dishonoured his parents by smiting them was to be put to death! (See Exo. 21:15).

(6) *Not kill* (v. 13). Death was the penalty for killing another person according to Exo. 21:12-14.

(7) *No adultery* (v. 14). According to Lev. 20:10 both the adulterer and the adulteress were to be put to death!

(8) *Not steal* (v.15). In the case of a man stealing another man, death was the penalty according to Exo. 21:16. In some cases, a thief would be sold and in other cases restitution (sometimes as much as five for one) would be made. (See Exo. 21:16 and 22:1-14).

(9) Not *bear false witness against neighbor* (v. 16). It seems from a reading of Deut. 19:16-21 that death could be exacted as a penalty in some cases but not in most cases.

(10) **Not covet** (v. 17). Although death is not specifically stated as a penalty for a violation of this commandment, covetousness could lead to violations of other commandments which could (and in many cases would) result in death! Achan in Joshua 7 is an example of this.

Yes, without question, **the Law that contained the ten commandments was a law of death!**

THE SAME LAW (THE OLD TESTAMENT) THAT CONTAINED THE TEN COMMANDMENTS ALSO CONTAINED A NUMBER OF OTHER COMMANDMENTS THAT HAD DEATH PENALTIES FOR THOSE WHO VIOLATED THEM. Here are some examples.

1. Lev. 20:15- **"And if a man lie with a beast, he shall surely be put to death: and ye shall slay the beast."** (Cf. Exo. 22:19).

2. Read Deut. 13:5 and you will see that a false prophet or a dreamer of dreams was to be put to death! NOTE: Suppose all false prophets today were put to death. It might be good for the people but it would be sad because false prophets will be lost eternally in hell!

3. Exo. 22:18- **"Thou shalt not suffer a witch to live."** (Also read Lev. 20:27).

4. Read Lev. 18:22 & 20:13 and you will see that those guilty of homosexuality were to be put to death.

5. According to Deut. 21:18-21 a stubborn and rebellious son that was a drunkard and a glutton was to be

put to death.

NOTE: The evidence is overwhelmlng! The conclusion is clear! The Law that God gave through Moses to
Israel that contained the ten commandments *was a law of
death!* It required the death penalty for many of its
violations. We should rejoice and be grateful that we are
not under that Law today. We are under *truth and grace!*

VII. THE FIRST COVENANT (INCLUDING THE
TEN COMMANDMENTS) WAS FAULTY. Although
Sabbatarians deny this fact the Hebrew writer says: **"For if
that first covenant had been faultless, then should no place
have been sought for the second."** (8:7). Although the first
covenant was perfect in the sense that it accomplished that
which God designed it to accomplish, it was faulty from
other standpoints. Let us consider some ways in which it
was faulty.

1. *Although it purified the flesh, it did not purify
the conscience.* (See Heb. 9:13-14)

2. *Since the ceremonies, etc., were required in
the tabernacle and later in the temple,* it could not be a
worldwide religion.

3. *Its promises emphasized the physical and
temporal rather than the spiritual and eternal.*

4. *It could not permanently take away sin.* (See
Heb. 10:4).

5. *Under it violators died without mercy.* (See
Heb. 10:28).

6. *The law **made nothing perfect** (*according to
Heb. 7:19), **"but the bringing in of a better hope did; by the
which we draw nigh unto God."**

*Yes, the first covenant was **faulty**, but the second is*

81

a perfect law of liberty! (Cf. James 1:25).

VIII. SABBATARIANS OFTEN ASSERT THAT "WE MAY STEAL, KILL, COMMIT ADULTERY, CO-VET. ETC. IF WE ARE NOT UNDER THE TEN COMMANDMENT LAW TODAY THAT GOD GAVE TO ISRAEL THROUGH MOSES."

 1. Although it is often asserted, it is never proven!

 2. Sin is a transgression of God's law according to 1 John 3:4. Adam transgressed God's law by eating of the forbidden fruit (cf. Gen. 2:16-17; 3:1-6) *before* God gave the ten commandment law to Israel through Moses. (See Exo. 20:1-17; Deut. 5:1-22). The commandment that Adam violated was *not* one of the ten commandments! Thus sin entered the world *before* the giving of the ten commandment law to Israel!

 3. After the giving of the ten commandment law by Moses to Israel and after it was fulfilled, nailed to the cross and taken out of the way (as taught in Mt. 5:17-18; Luke 24:44-46; Col. 2:14-17; etc.), Simon sinned by trying to buy the power like the apostles had to impart the Holy Ghost to others (in a miraculous way). (See Acts 8:14-24). NOTE: Simon did not sin by violating one of the ten commandments.

 Let us now consider the ten commandments as contained in the law God gave to Israel by Moses and notice how the New Testament Scriptures prohibit or enjoin every thing (and more) that was prohibited or enjoined by the ten commandment law except the command to keep the sabbath day holy. The New Testament

does not command sabbath keeping.

A. The ten commandment law taught *no other gods before God*. (Cf. Exo. 20:3). 'The New Testament teaches that *we should turn from vanities unto the living God* that made heaven, earth and sea and all things therein. (See Acts 14:15).

B. The ten commandment law taught *no graven images, etc.* (Cf. Exo. 20:4-5). The New Testament teaches that *we should keep ourselves from idols*. (See I John 5:21).

C. The ten commandment law said: **"Thou shalt not take the name of the Lord thy God in vain."** (Cf. Exo. 20:7). The New Testament *forbids swearing and blasphemy* and teaches us that we will give an account for every idle word that we speak. (See James 5:12; Col. 3:8 & Mt. 12:34-37).

D. The ten commandment law said: **"Honour thy mother and thy father..."** (Cf. Exo. 20:12. The New Testament teaches *children to obey and honour their parents* in Eph. 6:1-3 and in I Tim. 5:4 we are taught to show piety at home and to requite our parents.

E. The ten commandment law said: **"Thou shalt not kill"** (Exo. 20:13). The New Testament teaches us *that murder is a work of the flesh* and *those who commit murder cannot inherit the kingdom of heaven.* (See Gal. 5:i9-21). It also teaches us *to love the brethren, our neighbors and our enemies* (1 Thess. 4:9; I John 2:10; 3:14; Rom. 13:8-10; Mt. 5:43-48). *None of these were found in the ten commandments*.

NOTE: The commandment that prohibited bearing false witness against the neighbor and coveting anything that belongs to the neighbor did not teach the Israelites love him. Other commandments in the Law of Moses (the first covenant) did teach them to love their neighbors. (Cf. Lev. 19:18).

F. The ten commandment law said: **"Thou shalt not commit adultery"** (Exo. 20:14). The New Testament *not only forbids adultery but also forbids looking on a woman to lust after her and also calls that adultery*. (See Mt. 5:27-28). Adultery is a work of the flesh according to Gal. 5:19-21. Also see Mark 7:20-23.

G. The ten commandment law said: **"Thou shalt not steal"** (Exo. 20:15). The New Testament teaches us *not to steal* (See Eph. 4:28). The New Testament teaches us to **"give to him that needeth"** in that same passage. Which of the ten commandments taught the Israelites to **"give to him that he needeth"**?

H. The ten commandment law said: **"Thou shalt not bear false witness against thy neighbour"** (Exo. 20:16). The New Testament teaches us *not to lie which includes bearing false witness against our neighbor. It also includes bearing false witness against our enemy or about anything else. Lying in all forms* is condemned in the New Testament. (See Col. 3:9; Eph. 4:25; Rev.21: 8; 21:27).

I. The ten commandment law **prohibited the Israelite from coveting his neighbour's wife or possessions.** (Cf. Exo. 20:17). The New Testament teaches **us not to covet and tells us that covetousness is idolatry**. It also teaches us that the covetous shall not inherit the kingdom of heaven. (Sec Eph. 5:3-5; Col. 3:5). Which of the ten commandments prohibited the Israelite from coveting the wife and possessions of his enemy?

NOTE: People today do not sin by violating the ten

commandments as such, but by violating the law of Christ as revealed in the New Testament. *No, we are not under the ten commandments today! Yes, it is sinful to steal, kill, commit adultery, covet, bear false witness against our neighbor, etc.*

IX. COMMANDMENTS OF GOD GIVEN TO OTHERS IN A PRIOR DISPENSATION ARE NOT BINDING ON US TODAY.

A. This is a basic principle of truth that many religionists over look. They assume (and assert) without proof from the Scriptures that all of God's commandments apply to all people of all ages.

B. Let us consider some commandments that God gave in prior dispensations that will illustrate the above principle.

1. God commanded Adam not to eat of the fruit of the tree of knowledge of good and evil in Gen. 2:16-17. This command does *not* apply to us in this dispensation!

2. God commanded Noah to build an ark of gopher wood in Gen. 6:14. This command does *not* apply to us in this age!

3. God commanded Abram to offer his son Isaac for a burnt offering in Gen. 22:2. This command does *not* apply to us in this age!

4. God commanded Moses to number the firstborn among the Israelites in Num. 3:42. This command does *not* apply to us in this dispensation!

5. God commanded Aaron to offer burnt offerings and sin offerings, etc. in Lev. 9:7. This command

85

does *not* apply to us in this age!

6. God commanded Joshua to set the city of Ai on fire in Joshua 8:8. This command does *not* apply to us in this dispensation!

7. God commanded the Israelites to **"Remember the sabbath day, to keep it holy"** in Exo. 20:8. That command (like the other above ones) does *not* apply to us in this dispensation! It was given to the children of Israel in a prior dispensation! It was not given for people who live in the gospel dispensation! We are under law to Christ!

X. MISCELLANEOUS FACTS TO CONSIDER IN LIGHT OF GOD'S WORD!

A. In Col. 2:14-17 in the context of judging us **"in meat, or in drink, or in respect of an holy day, or of the new moon, or of the sabbath days"**, Paul tells us that the handwriting of ordinances that was against us was blotted out, taken out of the way and nailed to the cross. NOTE: *This included the sabbath!*

Someone might ask: How could the sabbath law be against us? Here are some ways.

(1) *It forbids kindling a fire on the sabbath* even in sub-zero weather. Exo. 35:3 says: **"Ye shall kindle no fire throughout your habitations upon the sabbath day."**

(2) *It forbids any boiling or baking on the sabbath*. Exo. 16:23 says: **"Tomorrow is the rest of the holy sabbath unto the Lord: bake that which ye will bake today, and seethe that ye will seethe."**

(3) *It forbids bearing any burden on the sabbath* which would include carrying books, maps, chalk,

86

erasers, yardsticks, etc. to (or in) schools (or to or in assemblies) on the sabbath. Jer. 17:21-22 says: **"...bear no burden on the sabbath day, nor bring it in by the gates of Jerusalem; Neither carry forth a burden out of your houses on the sabbath day."**

(4) *It requires the offering of two lambs every sabbath*. Numbers 28:9 says: **"And on the sabbath day two lambs of the first year without spot..."**

(5) *It requires the death of those who violate it*. Exo. 31:14-15 says: **"Ye shall keep the sabbath therefore: for it is holy unto you: everyone that defileth it shall surely be put to death: for whosoever doeth any work...in the sabbath day, he shall surely be put to death."** NOTE: Yes, the sabbath law, if in effect, would be against us even more so than meat, drink, an holy day, or the new moon, etc.

B. SOME INTERESTING FACTS TO CONSIDER

(1) The word translated *"sabbath"* is purely a Hebrew word that is never found in the Old Testament till the time of Moses. (Cf. Exo. 16:23).

(2) Neither the expression *"the moral law"* nor *"the ceremonial law"* is found in the Scriptures. Nor can we find the expression *"temporal law"* or *"eternal law"* in the Scriptures! NOTE: These expressions are often used by Sabbatarians to make distinctions in God's law, the Old Covenant where such distinctions do not exist.

(3) The *"sabbath"* is not even mentioned in twenty-four of the thirty nine books of the Old Testament Scriptures. Neither is it mentioned in twenty-one of the twenty-seven books of the New Testament Scriptures.

(4) There is no record in the Old Testament of the sabbath being kept by *any* man or woman till the Jews (Israelites) kept it as recorded in Exo. 16-20.

(5) The sabbath law was given to the Israelites, not to any other nation as such. Referring to the Israelites, God said: **"I gave them my sabbaths..."** (Ezekiel 20:12).

(6) Speaking of the Israelites, God said: **"...I will also cause her mirth to cease, her feast days, her new moons, and her sabbaths, and all her solemn feasts."** (Hosea 2:11). God called the sabbaths *"her sabbaths."* Also observe the fact that God said He would cause *her* sabbaths to cease along with her mirth, feast days, new moons and solemn feasts. NOTE: This statement was made more than seven hundred years before the New Covenant became in effect (or in force) in the first century. So God did cause *"her sabbaths"* to cease as promised.

(7) If the first Covenant was intended for all people (Israelites and people of all other nations as Sabbatarians claim) isn't it rather strange that Jesus said, **"I am not sent but unto the lost sheep of the house of Israel"** in Mt. 15:24? Also isn't it strange that while under the *first Covenant* that Jesus commanded the apostles, saying, **"Go not into the way of the Gentiles, and into any city of the Samaritans enter ye not: But go rather to the lost sheep of the house of Israel"** in Mt. 10:5-6? NOTE: Under the *New Covenant* the gospel was to be preached to every creature in all the world. (See Mk. 16:15-16; Mt. 28:19; Lk. 24:47).

(8). Sabbatarians claim that the sabbath is to be observed in this gospel age because God said the sabbath **"is a sign between me and the children of Israel for ever..."** in Exo. 31:17. Speaking of a servant who wanted to remain

88

with his master after serving him six years, Exo. 21:6 says: **"...and he shall serve him for ever."** NOTE: We have the same word both in the English and the original language. The Sabbatarians would like for the word (*forever* in Exo. 21:6) to mean *age lasting* so that servitude would come to an end, but they would like for the *same word* (in Exo. 31:17) to mean *endless* so that the sabbath continues to be in force. There is no justification for the different meanings being applied to this word in these passages. To assume and assert things is not proof of such! It is the same word in the original language as well as in the English version.

(9) If the sabbath had been kept by Abraham (as some Sabbatarians claim), or even by the Israelites while they were in Egypt, isn't it rather strange that about 2500 years later the Israelites did not know what punishment to exact when one violated the sabbath law as shown in Numbers 15:34? You would certainly think that the penalty for violating the sabbath command would have been known along with the command to keep the sabbath holy.

(10) If the sabbath was observed by men (the "patriarchs") such as Adam, Enoch, Noah, Abraham, Isaac, Jacob, etc. and others over a period of about 2500 years before Moses, isn't it strange that *there is no inspired record* of such taking place. Why would anyone even think about suggesting that it was in the absence of a divine record?

YOU CANNOT PICK AND CHOOSE

Sabbatarians would like to pick and choose what they want that was given to people who lived under a prior dispensation and a different covenant. However, if you are under one command of the old Law, you are under all! (See Gal. 3:10; 5:2-3). If you choose to bind the sabbath, to be consistent you must also bind circumcision, burnt sacrifices, meat offerings, incense, the passover, the feast of tabernacles, new moons and the death penalty for those who violate the sabbath law. (See John 7:22-23; Exo. 20:7-10; Lev. 23;1-44; Psa. 81:3; 31:14-15).

If you choose to bind any of the old Law (for example, circumcision), **"Christ shall profit you nothing."** (Gal. 5:2). If you choose to bind *any* part of the old Law (circumcision, for example), you are **"a debtor to do the whole law."** (Gal. 5:3). If you are justified by the law, Christ has become of no effect to you and **"ye are fallen from grace"**! (Cf. Gal. 5:4). NOTE: The same principle would apply to "sabbath keeping." If you choose to bind "sabbath keeping", **"Christ shall profit you nothing."** If you choose to bind "sabbath keeping", you are **"a debtor to do the whole law."** If you are justified by the law (which includes "sabbath keeping), Christ has become of no effort to you and **"ye are fallen from grace"**! Clear and simple to truth seekers.

No, the sabbath law is not binding on Christians today! Don't be deceived by false teachers! If you are among those who believe that the sabbath law is binding on Christians today, may God bless each of you as you give diligence in your studies of the Scriptures. We sincerely plead with you to give up that false teaching and accept the truth as revealed in the Scriptures! There is absolutely *no Scriptural proof* that God ever intended that the *"sabbath command"* be a part of the *New Covenant of Jesus Christ* that was ratified with His precious blood. We have no right to assume that "sabbath keeping" in the Gospel age will be pleasing to God. *You must accept the truth as revealed in the Scriptures (*properly divided– see 2 Tim. 2:15) *to be saved!*

THE FIRST DAY OF THE WEEK

In Mark 16:9 we read: **"Now when Jesus was risen early the first day of the week, he appeared first to Mary Magdalene, out of whom he had cast seven devils."** NOTE: Without question, Jesus was raised on *the first day of the week!* In John 20:19 we read: **"Then the same day at evening, being the first day of the week, when the doors were shut where the disciples were assembled for fear of the Jews, came Jesus and stood in the midst, and saith unto them, Peace be unto you."** NOTE: This appearance of Jesus to His disciples occurred on *the first day of the week!*

After the day of Pentecost (the day of the beginning of the NT church) in Acts 2, we find only two passages in which the expression *"the first day of the week"* appears. Here they are: (1) Acts 20:7- **"And upon the first day of the week, when the disciples came together to break bread, Paul preached unto them, ready to depart on the morrow; and continued his speech until midnight."** NOTE: Obviously the expression *break (ing- ed) bread* as used in this verse stands for or suggests the Lord's Supper. This is a *divinely approved example* of it being observed on the first day of the week. We follow that example. (2) 1 Cor. 16:2- **"Upon the first day of the week let every one of you lay by him in store, as God hath prospered him, that there be no gatherings when I come."** NOTE: The giving (laying by of our means) into a collection for the saints was to be done *on the first day of the week.* NOTE: We follow that example in giving into a common fund or treasury in the local church to finance its work.

In Rev. 1:10 John the Revelator said: **"I was in the Spirit on the Lord's day..."** NOTE: The resurrection of Jesus

Christ occurred on *the first day of the week.* The disciples at Troas met upon *the first day of the week* to break bread and saints were commanded to lay by in store *upon the first day of the week.* We also find expressions like *"the Lord's table"* (see 1 Cor. 10:21), *"the Lord's supper"* (see 1 Cor. 11:20), *"the Lord's death"* (see 1 Cor. 11:26) and *"the Lord's body"* (see 1 Cor. 11:29). These things belonged to the Lord in a special way.

FURTHER NOTE: These things may suggest that John had reference to *the first day of the week* when he said, *I was in the Spirit on the Lord's day.*

OBSERVATION: As far as I have been able to find out, the sabbath is *never* referred to in either Old or New Testaments as *the Lord's Day* unless it is here in Rev. 1:10. There is no evidence that the sabbath is referred to here. Since it is not referred to as the Lord's day in the OT, there is no reason for us to assume that it is here either since this occurred years after the gospel age began. *The sabbath law* had been abrogated at the cross. (See Col. 2:14-17).

Please *examine your hearts and search your souls* in light of what the Word of God says and *make sure that you have a sincere love of the truth.* (See 2 Thess. 2:9-14; Mt. 5:6). Otherwise you can not be saved in heaven. **"Study to show thyself approved unto God, a workman that needeth not to be ashamed, rightly dividing the Word of truth."** You will face *the truth as revealed in the Scriptures* (properly divided) in the day of judgment!

Send all questions, comments or criticisms
to

Carrol Ray Sutton
1103 Edmondson Street
Albertville, Alabama 35950